MAE
WEST

AMERICAN WOMEN of ACHIEVEMENT

MAE WEST

CAROL BERGMAN

CHELSEA HOUSE PUBLISHERS

NEW YORK • NEW HAVEN • PHILADELPHIA

EDITOR-IN-CHIEF: Nancy Toff
EXECUTIVE EDITOR: Remmel T. Nunn
MANAGING EDITOR: Karyn Gullen Browne
COPY CHIEF: Juliann Barbato
ART DIRECTOR: Giannella Garrett
MANUFACTURING MANAGER: Gerald Levine

Staff for MAE WEST:

TEXT EDITOR: Marian W. Taylor
ASSISTANT EDITOR: Maria Behan
EDITORIAL ASSISTANT: Karen Schimmel
COPYEDITORS: Gillian Bucky, Sean Dolan, Ellen Scordato
PICTURE RESEARCHER: Eleanor Porter
DESIGNER: Design Oasis
PRODUCTION COORDINATOR: Laura McCormick
COVER ILLUSTRATION: Donna Day

CREATIVE DIRECTOR: Harold Steinberg

3 5 7 9 8 6 4 2

Library of Congress Cataloging in Publication Data

Bergman, Carol. MAE WEST

(American women of achievement)
Bibliography: p.
Includes index.
1. West, Mae—Juvenile literature. 2. Entertainers—United
States—Biography—Juvenile literature. [1. West, Mae. 2. Actors
and actresses. 3. Entertainers.] I. Title. II. Series.
PN2287.W4566B4   1987   791.43′028′0924 [B] [92]   87-738

ISBN 1-55546-681-8

C O N T E N T S

"Remember the Ladies"—Matina S. Horner 7

1. "I Was an Original" 13

2. Brooklyn Childhood 19

3. The Vaudeville Years 29

4. Playwright 39

5. Hollywood Goddess 53

6. Troubled Waters 69

7. Return to the Stage.......................87

8. The Last Years 97

Further Reading 106

Chronology 107

Index 108

AMERICAN WOMEN of ACHIEVEMENT

Abigail Adams
women's rights activist

Jane Addams
social worker

Louisa May Alcott
author

Marian Anderson
singer

Susan B. Anthony
woman suffragist

Ethel Barrymore
actress

Clara Barton
founder of the American Red Cross

Elizabeth Blackwell
physician

Nellie Bly
journalist

Margaret Bourke-White
photographer

Pearl Buck
author

Rachel Carson
biologist and author

Mary Cassatt
painter

Agnes De Mille
choreographer

Emily Dickinson
poet

Isadora Duncan
dancer

Amelia Earhart
aviator

Mary Baker Eddy
founder of the Christian Science church

Betty Friedan
feminist

Althea Gibson
tennis champion

Emma Goldman
revolutionary

Helen Hayes
actress

Lillian Hellman
playwright

Katharine Hepburn
actress

Karen Horney
psychoanalyst

Anne Hutchinson
religious leader

Mahalia Jackson
gospel singer

Helen Keller
humanitarian

Jeane Kirkpatrick
diplomat

Emma Lazarus
poet

Clare Boothe Luce
author and diplomat

Barbara McClintock
biologist

Margaret Mead
anthropologist

Edna St. Vincent Millay
poet

Julia Morgan
architect

Grandma Moses
painter

Louise Nevelson
sculptor

Sandra Day O'Connor
Supreme Court Justice

Georgia O'Keeffe
painter

Eleanor Roosevelt
diplomat and humanitarian

Wilma Rudolph
champion athlete

Florence Sabin
physician

Beverly Sills
singer

Gertrude Stein
author

Gloria Steinem
feminist

Harriet Beecher Stowe
author and abolitionist

Mae West
entertainer

Edith Wharton
author

Phillis Wheatley
poet

Babe Zaharias
champion athlete

CHELSEA HOUSE PUBLISHERS

"Remember the Ladies"

MATINA S. HORNER

Remember the Ladies." That is what Abigail Adams wrote to her husband John, then a delegate to the Continental Congress, as the Founding Fathers met in Philadelphia to form a new nation in March of 1776. "Be more generous and favorable to them than your ancestors. Do not put such unlimited power in the hands of the Husbands. If particular care and attention is not paid to the Ladies," Abigail Adams warned, "we are determined to foment a Rebellion, and will not hold ourselves bound by any Laws in which we have no voice, or Representation."

The words of Abigail Adams, one of the earliest American advocates of women's rights, were prophetic. Because when we have not "remembered the ladies," they have, by their words and deeds, reminded us so forcefully of the omission that we cannot fail to remember them. For the history of American women is as interesting and varied as the history of our nation as a whole. American women have played an integral part in founding, settling, and building our country. Some we remember as remarkable women who—against great odds—achieved distinction in the public arena: Anne Hutchinson, who in the 17th century became a charismatic religious leader; Phillis Wheatley, an 18th-century black slave who became a poet; Susan B. Anthony, whose name is synonymous with the 19th-century women's rights movement, and who led the struggle to enfranchise women; and, in our own century, Amelia Earhart, the first woman to cross the Atlantic Ocean by air.

These extraordinary women certainly merit our admiration, but other women, "common women," many of them all but forgotten, should also be recognized for their contributions to American thought and culture. Women have been community builders; they have founded schools and formed voluntary associations to help those in need; they have assumed the major responsibility for rearing children, passing on from one generation to the next the values that keep a culture alive. These and innumerable other contributions, once ignored, are now being recognized by scholars, students, and the public. It is exciting and gratifying to realize that a part of our history that was hardly acknowledged a few generations ago is now being studied and brought to light.

In recent decades, the field of women's history has grown from obscurity to a politically controversial splinter movement to academic respectability, in many cases mainstreamed into such traditional disciplines as history, economics, and psychology. Scholars of women, both female and male, have organized research centers at such prestigious institutions as Wellesley College, Stanford University, and the University of California. Other notable centers for women's studies are the Center for the American Woman and Politics at the Eagleton Institute of Politics at Rutgers University; the Henry A. Murray Research Center for the Study of Lives, at Radcliffe College; and the Women's Research and Education Institute, the research arm of the Congressional Caucus on Women's Issues. Other scholars and public figures have established archives and libraries, such as the Schlesinger Library on the History of Women in America, at Radcliffe College, and the Sophia Smith Collection, at Smith College, to collect and preserve the written and tangible legacies of women.

From the initial donation of the Women's Rights Collection in 1943, the Schlesinger Library grew to encompass vast collections documenting the manifold accomplishments of American women. Simultaneously, the women's movement in general and the academic discipline of women's studies in particular also began with a narrow definition and gradually expanded their mandate. Early causes such as woman suffrage and social reform, abolition and organized labor were joined by newer concerns such as the history of women in business and the professions and in politics and government; the study of the family; and social issues such as health policy and education.

Women, as historian Arthur M. Schlesinger, jr., once pointed out, "have constituted the most spectacular casualty of traditional history. They have made up at least half the human race, but you could never tell that by looking at the books historians write." The new breed of historians is remedying that omission. They have written books about immigrant women and about working-class women who struggled for survival in cities and about black women who met the challenges of life in rural areas. They are telling the stories of women who, despite the barriers of tradition and economics, became lawyers and doctors and public figures.

The women's studies movement has also led scholars to question traditional interpretations of their respective disciplines. For example, the study of war has traditionally been an exercise in military and political analysis, an examination of strategies planned and executed by men. But scholars of women's history have pointed out that wars have also been periods of tremendous change and even opportunity for women, because the very absence of men on the home front enabled them to expand their educational, economic, and professional activities and to assume leadership in their homes.

The early scholars of women's history showed a unique brand of courage in choosing to investigate new subjects and take new approaches to old ones. Often, like their subjects, they endured criticism and even ostracism by their academic colleagues. But their efforts have unquestionably been worthwhile, because with the publication of each new study and book another piece of the historical patchwork is sewn into place, revealing an increasingly comprehensive picture of the role of women in our rich and varied history.

Such books on groups of women are essential, but books that focus on the lives of individuals are equally indispensable. Biographies can be inspirational, offering their readers the example of people with vision who have looked outside themselves for their goals and have often struggled against great obstacles to achieve them. Marian Anderson, for instance, had to overcome racial bigotry in order to perfect her art and perform as a concert singer. Isadora Duncan defied the rules of classical dance to find true artistic freedom. Jane Addams had to break down society's notions of the proper role for women in order to create new social institutions, notably the settlement house. All of these women had to come to terms both with themselves and with the world in which they lived. Only then could they move ahead as pioneers in their chosen callings.

Biography can inspire not only by adulation but also by realism. It helps us to see not only the qualities in others that we hope to emulate, but also, perhaps, the weaknesses that made them "human." By helping us identify with the subject on a more personal level they help us to feel that we, too, can achieve such goals. We read about Eleanor Roosevelt, for instance, who occupied a unique and seemingly enviable position as the wife of the president. Yet we can sympathize with her inner dilemma: an inherently shy woman, she had to force herself to live a most public life in order to use her position to benefit others. We may not be able to imagine ourselves having the immense poetic talent of Emily Dickinson, but from her story we can understand the challenges faced by a creative woman who was expected to fulfill many family responsibilities. And though few of us will ever reach the level of athletic accomplishment displayed by Wilma Rudolph or Babe Zaharias, we can still appreciate their spirit, their overwhelming will to excel.

A biography is a multifaceted lens. It is first of all a magnification, the intimate examination of one particular life. But at the same time, it is a wide-angle lens, informing us about the world in which the subject lived. We come away from reading about one life knowing more about the social, political, and economic fabric of the time. It is for this reason, perhaps, that the great New England essayist Ralph Waldo Emerson wrote, in 1841, "There is properly no history: only biography." And it is also why biography, and particularly women's biography, will continue to fascinate writers and readers alike.

MAE
WEST

A kidnap victim is carried aloft in Rescued From the Eagle's Nest, *an early Edison thriller. The first movies, known as "flickers," were only about five minutes long.*

ONE

"I Was an Original"

"Come up and see me some time." Most people have heard that line, and many know it was spoken by an actress named Mae West. Few people today, however, know very much about West, although her spectacular career, which began in 1900, continued until just before her death in 1980 at the age of 87.

Mae West's life spanned two centuries, two world wars, and countless technological, social, and cultural changes. On December 8, 1895, the first motion pictures were shown in Paris, France. The work of French photographic pioneers Auguste and Louis Lumière, this primitive movie showed workers emerging from a factory. Four months later, flickering images of dancing girls and ocean waves were projected on a screen in New York City by American inventor Thomas Alva Edison's new machine, the kineto-scope. Mae West was then three years old. Four years later, she began her theatrical career.

By 1932, when West made her first movie, the film industry had established itself in Hollywood, California. Here, most of the actresses and actors worked as "contract players"—glorified laborers—for such huge motion picture studios as Paramount, Universal, and Metro-Goldwyn-Mayer. Many of these performers—young men and women with beautiful faces—drifted into obscurity after making only one or two films.

Mae West, however, was different. Along with a handful of other superstars of the day—Marlene Dietrich, Greta Garbo, Jean Harlow—West had staying power. She was not the first "sex goddess" or "blond bombshell" to appear in Hollywood, and she was not even the most popular of these great

An 1896 wrestling match is preserved for posterity in a film made by Thomas Alva Edison. Edison, who had invented the light bulb in 1879, was among the world's first moviemakers.

Mary Pickford displays the charm that made her "America's Sweetheart" in the 1920s. Despite her look of girlish innocence, Pickford was among Hollywood's shrewdest businesswomen.

stars. But she was undoubtedly the most independent and powerful woman in Hollywood.

West earned more money and had more control over the scripts, casting, and crew of her films than any other actor or actress of her time. Not even Mary Pickford, who was known as "America's Sweetheart," and who was a cofounder of Universal Pictures, had as much authority on the set as West. "Never before, and never since," says film historian Marjorie Rosen in her book, *Popcorn Venus*, "has a woman in films been so thoroughly in control of her destiny."

Mae West knew how to market her own image, and she marketed it unceasingly. In her more than 70 years in show business, she was rarely without work, a claim that can be made by few entertainers, even the most successful.

West loved to work, and was, in fact, never idle. There was always a new project to think about, another play or movie script to write, a new song to learn. Although she was very fond of sweets, she drank no alcohol and became interested in the benefits of health food long before it became fashionable. Her personal life was highly disciplined, but her stage and screen image—which she had deliberately created—was that of a wild and dissipated woman.

Like Mae West, Marlene Dietrich was one of the screen's most durable "sex goddesses." Her air of sophisticated mystery, however, was the exact opposite of West's frankly sensual image.

The roles that West sought out and wrote for herself were usually those of "loose" women. It was, furthermore, common knowledge that she had many lovers until she settled down to live with one man at the age of 65. Nevertheless, work was always the center of her life, and she bristled at the thought of being regarded as an immoral person. Decades before the women's movement, she claimed the right to be respected for what she was:

a woman who liked men but had no need for a man's financial support—or wedding ring.

West worked hard on what she called the "Mae West Character"—a sultry, hip-swinging blond with few inhibitions. Although unblushingly sensual, that character was also richly comic. "My original impression of Mae," said an old friend, writer Marion Spitzer Thompson, "was that she believed all that sexy stuff about herself.

Sidonie-Gabrielle Colette, the popular French writer whose novels include Gigi *and* La Chatte (The Cat), *was among Mae West's many intellectual admirers.*

But she began to recognize the value of self-kidding and began broadening it into parody. I think that explains her enduring hold on people's imaginations."

West detested hypocrisy, particularly on the issue of sex. As a consequence, she was hounded by censors throughout her career. She stated her attitude toward the "forces of decency" in a *New Yorker* magazine interview in 1928. "Once [you] show people you're afraid," said the fearless West, "you're through, see?"

West successfully defied censorship from 1912 until 1933, when she made her third Hollywood film. At that point, rules established by the guardians of the public morals became so restrictive that the Mae West Character almost died. Old Hollywood observers shook their heads and wondered if any entertainment constructed along the lines of West's could survive the diligent censors.

West did manage to continue as a film star but, tightly controlled by the censors, her scripts lost much of the earthy humor for which they had been celebrated. Still, she kept on making movies, and people kept on paying to see them.

During West's early career, most of her fans were men, but as women became more confident of their independence, increasing numbers adopted West as their emblem. The French author Colette, a contemporary of West, wrote: "She alone, out of an enormous and dull catalog of heroines, does not get married at the end of the film, does not gaze sadly at her declining youth in a silver-framed mirror.... Can you honestly name another artist, male or female, in the cinema whose comic acting equals that of this ample blond who undulates in little waves, who is ornamental with her real diamonds, whose eye is pale and hard, whose throat swells with the coos of a professional dove?"

Film history offers no answer to Colette's question. Mae West was—as she was the first to admit—"an original."

West assumes a characteristic pose for a 1930s publicity photographer. The long gowns, elaborate jewelry, and enormous feathered hats of the Victorian age were her favorite clothes.

The "hourglass figures" featured in this 1900 magazine illustration were the era's ideal of feminine beauty. West often boasted that her mother had just such a "perfect" figure.

TWO

Brooklyn Childhood

Mary Jane West was born in Brooklyn, New York, on August 17, 1893. Queen Victoria was still on the throne of England, still setting the stern and "proper" tone of the era that bears her name. Victorian fashion dictated dark rooms crowded with massive furniture, tightly corseted and resolutely virtuous women, and a prim avoidance of any public mention of the human body.

The West household, established in a three-story brownstone house on Brooklyn's Bushwick Avenue, did not fit the Victorian mold. Its parlor was decorated in shades of turquoise, peach, and yellow. On its floors were colorful round rugs, and at its windows, billowing sheer curtains. In her later years, West often fondly recalled this house, whose airy brightness formed a sharp contrast to the shadowy clutter of the other homes in the neighborhood.

Mae West's childhood wardrobe reflected the same unconventional taste as her family's house. Instead of the somber, thick clothing worn by her friends, Mae wore pastel-colored dresses made of light and delicate fabrics. Everything she put on was designed and made by her mother, Matilda. "Tillie" West, who had studied fashion design and worked as a model before her marriage, loved clothes.

After she had become famous, Mae West regularly invented or exaggerated stories about her childhood and her parents' backgrounds. She always wrote her own scripts, so in a way, it was perfectly consistent for her to invent her own life story.

West sometimes described her mother as the descendant of an aristocratic French family; at other times, she said her mother had been born Mary Jane Copley, "related to the well-known Copleys of Boston." Tillie West,

European immigrants arrive in the United States in 1890. West's German-born mother had come to America in similar fashion, but West usually described her as a French aristocrat.

however, had been born Matilda Delker Doelger in Bavaria, Germany. The Doelgers had emigrated to the United States in 1882, and when Mae West was born, 11 years later, her mother still spoke with a marked German accent.

Strictly raised in an old-fashioned German household, Tillie West seems to have responded enthusiastically to the opportunities and freedom offered by the New World. She was remembered by her neighbors as an unconventional and sometimes aggressive woman—a description that might be regarded as a compliment in the 1980s, but one that was not especially flattering a century earlier.

Whatever the neighbors may have thought of Tillie West, Mae adored her "beautiful, charming, and refined" mother. She had, said her daughter, a "perfect" figure—perfection at the time consisting of voluptuous curves nipped in by a tiny waist. And Tillie West was irresistible to men. "There was a power and a vitality about Mother," West said in the autobiography she wrote in 1959, "that made a man melt before her glance."

Along with fine clothes, Tillie West liked elegant food and expensive furniture. She demanded "quality, quality, quality," reminisced her daughter. Tillie West's admiration for "quality" earned her a nickname from her husband: "Champagne Til." (Many years later, Mae West wrote and starred in *Diamond Lil*, a phenomenally successful musical that owed its title to this affectionate name for her mother.)

Mae's father, John Patrick West, was born in the United States to a family of Irish descent. Before he married Tillie Doelger, he had been a prizefighter, known locally as "Battling Jack, Champion of Brooklyn, New York." He was, said his daughter, a "rough lover of fun and fights" and a "wild, laughing man."

Mae West exaggerated her father's background, too, insisting that he had been "an epic figure" in Brooklyn. According to her, Jack West had once single-handedly captured two armed bank bandits and, on another occasion, avenged an insult to his wife by overcoming "100 angry men" in a saloon.

"Battling Jack" might not have been quite as formidable as his daughter claimed, but his violent temper frightened many people, including Mae. She never felt close to her father, whose "knobby muscles" and cigar-tinged breath struck her as anything but "refined."

In later years, Mae West conceded that her father had been a good provider and that he had never struck her or any other family member. A lifelong

"Baby Mae" was always her mother's favorite child. The little girl, who had charm, a pretty face — and a will of iron — usually managed to get what she wanted.

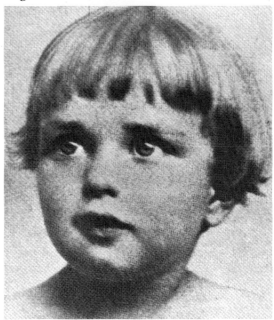

Carriages line the sidewalk in front of a late 19th-century livery stable. Such enterprises, one of which was operated by "Battling Jack" West, were common when Mae West was young.

boxing fan, she would finance the careers of many young fighters, perhaps paying unconscious tribute to "Battling Jack" West.

After his marriage, John West gave up fighting. He opened a livery stable, renting out horses and carriages and, in the winter, horse-drawn sleighs. His business did well, but when automobiles became popular, he gave it up and started a detective agency. Even-

tually, he entered the real estate business.

Until she was five years old, Mae was an only child. She and her mother often tried out new carriages John West was thinking of buying, and she would remember with pleasure their frequent rides through Brooklyn's leafy streets and parks. She particularly treasured the winter memory of riding in a sleigh, wrapped in furs as she

22

watched less fortunate pedestrians tramping through slush and mud. Like her mother, Mae West always had a taste for luxury.

Mae's sister, Mildred, was born in 1898. Just as Mary Jane had changed her name to Mae, Mildred became "Beverly" as soon as she was old enough to recognize a "dreary" name when she heard one. In 1899 the Wests became a family of five with the birth of John Edwin. Even after the arrival of her sister and brother, Mae remained her mother's favorite. She usually got her own way, a pattern that had been established early.

"Mae is a child that has to be humored and can't be forced or ordered," said Tillie West, according to her older daughter. "She resents even an unfavorable tone of voice." Mae West was always proud of the fact that, from an early age, she knew what she wanted. In her autobiography, *Goodness Had Nothing to Do With It*, she told a story that illustrates her strength of will at the age of four.

As a reward for having her picture taken, Mae had been promised a new doll by her mother. They went to the local department store and examined the tall shelf of dolls. Mae made her choice. Dressed in lilac, Mae's favorite color, it rested on the topmost shelf, high above the heads of the store's clerks. Because the dolls were identical except for the color of their dresses, Mae was asked if she would not be just as happy with one that could be easily reached. She would not.

"That one," she said, pointing firmly. "Only that one."

The store's manager finally ordered two male clerks to bring a tall ladder and fetch the doll. A crowd of customers watched as the determined little girl got what she wanted. Many parents might have found such behavior obnoxious; Mae's mother thought it was adorable.

"She tried in every way to understand me," wrote Mae West later, "and she succeeded. It was this deep, loving understanding as long as she lived that more than anything else helped and sustained me on my way to success." For the rest of her life, Tillie West was always nearby whenever her daughter needed her.

Mae's sister Beverly felt neglected because of her mother's devotion to Mae. She too wanted to be an entertainer, and she bitterly resented the fact that her sister got all the encouragement. Although Beverly would appear in several of Mae's later plays, the two never got along well.

In 1900, when Mae was seven, she announced that she wished to go to dancing school. Her father objected, but her mother—as usual—took Mae's side, and Mae enrolled in "Professor" Watts's academy of the dance. After a few weeks, Watts decided Mae was talented enough to enter an amateur show at Brooklyn's Royal Theater.

Straw-hatted men and long-skirted women stroll along Broadway in 1910. Magnetically attracted by the stage, West attended shows here whenever she had the chance.

John West had grudgingly consented to Mae's dancing lessons and to her appearance at the amateur show. But he regarded her first performance, West wrote later, as a "test." If she panicked or forgot her song, she could forget about any further stage appearances.

The Royal, one of the 2,000 U.S. theaters that featured vaudeville (variety stage shows) in the early 1900s, was huge; above the orchestra section were tiers of box seats and two balconies. Neither the size of the theater nor the fact that she would be performing with a 12-piece orchestra, however, daunted Mae in the least. On the night of her debut, she was excited and eager but not nervous. As she would later note,

"I've never had stage fright in my life."

Mae's father sat in the audience as her mother nervously helped her daughter backstage. When Mae saw the spotlight shining on the acts that preceded hers, she said to the stage manager, "I have to have a spotlight." He agreed, but when the master of ceremonies announced her act—"Baby Mae—Song and Dance"—the spotlight was aimed at the far side of the stage. Mae refused to move.

The orchestra played her introduction, but the spot stayed on the other side. Wondering what was going on, the audience began to get restless. Then they heard a child's voice shouting, "Where is *my* spotlight?"

"Walk out, Baby Mae," said a stagehand in a whisper. "He'll see you and move the spot on you."

In a voice that reached the topmost balcony, Mae responded, "He'd better. My father is Battling Jack!"

The audience laughed and applauded as Mae finally pranced onto the stage to sing "Movin' Day," followed by a tap dance. The crowd roared its approval; Baby Mae was a hit. She received a gold medal and, after the show, her father's permission to pursue a stage career.

John West's objections to his daughter's ambitions had been completely overcome. "If they could bottle nerve," he said, "she'd have more than Rockefeller has oil."

At the turn of the century, long before movie theaters began to sprout all over the country, vaudeville and amateur shows were the nation's favorite form of entertainment. Mae followed up on her success at the Royal Theater by appearing in one amateur show after another.

She enlarged her repertoire to include such popular songs as "Doin' the Grizzly Bear" and "My Mariooch-Make-Da-Hoochy-Ma-Coocha in Coney Island," a comic dialect number. Wanting to look taller than she was, she wore her mother's huge, feather-crowned hat. She prevented it from falling off by keeping one hand on the back of her head as she sang.

This stance, with her other hand resting on her hip, became her trademark. Audiences were amused by the little girl with the big hat and the surprisingly husky voice and self-confident air.

Both Mae's parents accompanied her on the amateur-night expeditions. "Mama, on these magic nights, would have my muff and my scarf," explained West later, "and Papa would be carrying my makeup, costume changes, and dance shoes." Peace settled briefly in the West household, largely because of John West's acceptance of his daughter's stage career.

Mae was fiercely ambitious. "I would," she wrote, "share a dressing room with the other amateurs, but already I secretly felt myself out of their class." She planned to be a star by the time she was 16. School bored her, and when she reached the third grade her parents allowed her to drop out. She received occasional lessons from a tutor, but her formal education was over by the time she was eight years old.

Mae was happiest at the theater, where she could watch the professionals do their acts for the vaudeville shows that usually followed amateur contests. She knew she would soon be one of them. "I had a rough, husky voice that struck audiences as funny coming from a little kid," she recalled later. "I always won first prize—unless, of course, some out-of-work ham was there posing as an amateur."

Mae did not have to wait long to enter the ranks of professional entertain-

At 15, West had the face and figure of a mature woman. It was at this age that she went on her first vaudeville tour, playing a country-girl role known in show business as a "Sis Hopkins."

ers. In 1901, after spending only one year on the amateur circuit, she was recruited by Hal Clarendon, manager of a stock company that played at Brooklyn's Gotham Theater. A stock company consists of a group of salaried, full-time actors who appear in a rotating sequence of plays from their repertoire, or list, of selections.

Clarendon hired eight-year-old Mae to play children's parts in English "drawing-room" comedies and dramas. These plays had complicated plots about, said West later, "lost heirs, lost virtue, schoolboys in love with their aunts, seduced barmaids, and old lords killed in locked rooms."

If the play of the week had no child's part, Mae would sit in the theater and watch the other actors rehearse. "No actress," she said later, "ever had a better school." She stayed at the Gotham until she was 11; by then she was too physically mature to play children's roles.

During the next two years, Mae's only theatrical job was a short stint with an acrobatic troupe. Her job was to give the impression she was lifting a 500-pound weight and supporting the weight of three men. She later said that her work with the acrobats taught her how to maintain her figure by weight lifting.

Mae eagerly read all the news about the current stars of vaudeville, and she went to the theater as often as she could. When she was 15, Willie Hogan, an actor and old friend of the West family, asked her to join him on a tour. Hogan had a popular "kid act," a comedy routine in which he dressed as a country boy and regaled audiences with barnyard-inspired humor.

As part of Hogan's act, Mae played an innocent country girl who wore a sunbonnet and lace-trimmed bloomers and screamed in mock outrage at her boyfriend's jokes. Beneath the unsophisticated stage character, however, an independent and determined woman was developing.

Brooklyn's Royal Theater, the scene of Mae West's first public appearance, was one of thousands of U.S. vaudeville houses in the early 1900s. By 1930, movie palaces had replaced most of them.

Mae had always liked boys better than girls. As she put it in her autobiography, "Girls seemed a foolish investment of my time and boys could hold me up as I skated or assist me down from trolleys or wipe off park benches with their caps. They had such nice, hard biceps, too."

Soon after she got back from her tour with Hogan, Mae West met Joe Schenck, a good-looking 19-year-old whom she called "my first boyfriend with long trousers." Schenck, a talented piano player who had his own ragtime group, began bringing the six young men in his band to the Wests' house every Saturday night.

Tillie West thought Mae was too young to have a "steady beau," and she advised her daughter not to get too serious about Joe. It would be better, she said, if Mae saw other young men, too. Mae cheerfully accepted her mother's suggestion and was soon dating all the boys in the band.

Looking back on this period years later, West saw it as a turning point. It was the start of "the recurring pattern of multiple men in my life," as she put it in her autobiography.

With her natural flair for combining facts and wisecracks, she wrote, "I start with one, and usually five or six more put in an appearance. It's a satisfactory pattern. Getting down to your last man must be as bad as getting down to your last dollar." Mae West may not have been the most elegant stylist in American letters, but she was certainly among the most candid.

Heavily made up, a teenaged West adopts her best "vamp" expression for a publicity photograph. She worked hard to create the persona that she ultimately called the "Mae West Character."

THREE

The Vaudeville Years

During the years between 1910 and 1920, Mae West polished both her stage personality and her skills as a businesswoman. This was the decade just before the electronic revolution that changed the meaning of the word "entertainment." Film and radio were still in their infancy, and television was a distant dream.

The vaudeville stage was booming, and competition for a place in the spotlight was fierce. West knew that if she wanted to work, she would have to develop an image that would make her stand out among other performers.

No one who had known Mae West as a child star doubted the force of her ambition. Also evident from her early years was her talent for combining satire, burlesque, and vaudevillian song-and-dance routines. Still, she was not yet a unique stage presence, not yet the "fascinatin'" performer she was

sure she could be. She continued to tour with Willie Hogan and his "country boy" act. She was earning more money than most women her age, but she and Hogan were never reviewed by any important critics and she was far from satisfied.

In 1909, West and Hogan appeared in New York in a program that included a jazz dancer named Frank Wallace. The audience liked Wallace's routine. He received, in fact, much more applause than West and Hogan. West decided that Wallace had the makings of a star, and she asked him if he wanted to team up with her.

Dazzled by the performer he later described as "a slinky, peppy, classy little German girl," Wallace agreed; the two created an act that included such crowd-pleasing songs as "Lovin' Honey Man" and "Jealous."

Years afterward, Wallace recalled the

West was 17 when she became the wife of her vaudeville partner, Frank Wallace. The couple never lived together, but they remained legally married until 1942.

day when he and West auditioned for their first job as a duo. The theatrical booking agent, said Wallace, was not "bowled over" by their act, but he offered them $50 a week. They signed, but only after West had almost lost the engagement by calling the agent a "skinflint" and insisting that she and Wallace were worth more.

On their way out of the agent's office, Wallace questioned the wisdom of West's tactics. She refused to listen. "Let me be the business," she said. "You just play it straight." Her toughness made her no less attractive to Frank Wallace. He was in love, and he soon asked his 16-year-old partner to marry him.

Mae West was in love, too, but the object of her affections was the stage, not Frank Wallace. They took their act on the road, performing in New York, Pennsylvania, Ohio, Indiana, and Illinois. Wallace repeated his proposal at every stop. By the time they reached Milwaukee, Wisconsin, West was persuaded. She and Wallace were married by a city-court judge on April 11, 1911.

Frank Wallace was delighted, but his happiness was not to last. When the newlyweds returned to New York at the end of their tour, West told Wallace she did not want her parents to know she was married. They would, she said, have to live apart. He moved in with his sister, and she returned to her family in Brooklyn.

The marriage was over almost as

soon as it began; West never took Wallace seriously as a husband and never established a home with him. The couple eventually divorced, and West stayed single for the rest of her life.

West now set to work in earnest. Although she carefully studied the top stars of vaudeville, she would not copy anyone. She was going to create a stage character all her own, one that audiences could not fail to notice. She wanted to be the kind of performer people would remember long after they left the theater.

The key to the Mae West Character, which the actress would continue to develop for the next decade, was outrageousness. Female impersonators—men who performed in exaggerated, flamboyant women's dresses, heavy makeup, and piles of gaudy jewelry—were popular at the time, and West adapted some of their ideas.

She assembled the flashiest costumes her imagination could devise. A typical one was a purple evening gown, slit to the hip and accented with blazing "diamonds" and a fur piece dyed bright red. Topping off the outfit was a huge red hat crowned with waving ostrich plumes.

West created a new act to go with her colorful appearance. Aiming to be both sexy and funny, she would slither to center stage and belt out such tunes as "Isn't She a Brazen Thing?" and "It's an Awful Easy Way to Make a Living." In 1911, soon after she had drifted

Follies producer Florenz Ziegfeld examines photographs of aspiring chorus girls. *Constantly besieged by stagestruck women, he was astonished when West rejected his job offer.*

Gorgeously costumed showgirls form a tableau in the first production of Ziegfeld's Follies *in 1907. A new version of the popular revue appeared almost every year until 1931.*

away from Frank Wallace, she appeared at the Columbia Theater, a New York stage where new acts were often watched by booking agents and Broadway producers.

In the audience at the Columbia were two very important men. One was Florenz Ziegfeld, the famed producer whose annual *Follies* was a theatrical institution. The other man was Ned

Wayburn, a successful producer and director of Broadway musicals. Each asked West to come and talk to him after the show.

When she met with Ziegfeld, he offered her a job. She turned him down. She said his theater was too big, and the stage too far away from the audience. "I need people close to me," she explained. "The entire effect of my personality depends on audiences being able to see my facial expressions, gestures, slow, lazy comic mannerisms, to hear me properly." The astonished impresario suggested that West visit his theater; perhaps, he said, "You'll get used to the place."

West, however, had meant what she said. She went next to see Ned Wayburn, who asked her to appear in his upcoming musical, *A La Broadway*. She read the script and told Wayburn that she liked it, but that it needed a few revisions. The producer agreed, and West set to work writing new choruses for her principal number, a song called "They Are Irish."

West's additions to the song were in a variety of accents—English, Dutch, German, Italian, and Yiddish. Great waves of immigrants from Europe had arrived in the United States in the last half of the 19th century, and West believed that audiences would respond enthusiastically to her "melting-pot" lyrics. She was correct.

After the first performance, West was called back for seven encores. The New York theater critics were also impressed. The *Evening World* praised her "amusingly impudent manner," and *The New York Times* said that the "hitherto unknown" actress had a "snappy way of singing and dancing." Said the *Tribune*, "She has a bit of a sense of nonsense, which is the very latest addition to wit." Mae West had arrived in the theater.

Doing a turn as a male impersonator in 1916, West wears a top hat and dinner jacket. Although such acts were popular in vaudeville, the actress made only one appearance dressed as a man.

After *A La Broadway* ended its run, West went on tour with a new act. When she played in New Haven, Connecticut, in 1912, she had the first of what would be many battles with censorship.

She slinked onto the stage of New Haven's Palace Theater in furs and jewels, with slits up the side of her dress and a twinkle in her eye. The audience,

Yale men — sober and dignified in this formal portrait — responded to the closing of West's 1912 New Haven show by wrecking the theater. West called the destruction "a charming gesture."

many of whom were Yale students, went wild, but so did some of the city's more conservative citizens.

Lou Garvey, manager of the Palace, told West to tone down her show for the next performance. When she ignored his order, her engagement in New Haven was over. A local newspaper headlined the story: "Her Wriggles Cost Mae West Her Job: Curves in Motion Shock Lou Garvey at Palace; Whole Act Fired."

West enjoyed startling straitlaced people, but she was always proud of the fact that her material never contained vulgarity or "improper" lines or actions. "It wasn't what I did," she later said of the New Haven incident, "but how I did it. It wasn't what I said, but how I said it.... I had evolved into a symbol and didn't know it."

Undaunted by the closing of her show in New Haven, West finished her tour, wrote a new act, and opened in New York. She earned audience cheers and critical approval for her rendition of such tunes as "International Rag Song" and "Good Night, Nurse." By now, her provocative blend of extreme sensuality and good-humored comedy—a combination that would later be known as "camp"—had earned her

West tosses a smoldering look at the audience during a pre–World War I vaudeville performance. Her "femme fatale" routines were a deliberate mix of sensuality and self-parody.

West, who regarded herself as a true symbol of "liberty," said that during World War I she had put some "flag-waving" into her act to "match the torso waving."

a new label: "America's leading female impersonator." Increasingly, West was being recognized as a one-of-a-kind entertainer, exactly what she had set out to achieve.

From 1913 to 1916, West worked hard to advance her career. She traveled with her vaudeville act, always ready to tailor it to suit the tastes of different audiences. There was no Top 40 playlist in those years, and she relied on the stage manager in each city to tell her which songs were the most popular with the townspeople. She would conclude her performance with the local favorites. To open, she usually sang "I've Got a Style All My Own," a title that could have served as her slogan.

When the United States entered World War I in 1917, many vaudevillians took part in street-corner rallies where war bonds were sold, and many began to include patriotic songs in their repertoires. As for West: "I put some flag-waving into my act to match the torso waving." By this time, she had become one of the best known and most highly paid performers on the vaudeville circuit. Success, however, had not changed the personality of the outspoken and uninhibited actress.

"Most of us thought Mae was just shocking," said Helen Ford, an actress who starred with her in a 1918 musical called *Sometime*, "which was just what she wanted us to feel."

Actress Helen Ford was shocked by the uninhibited conversation of Mae West, her costar in 1918's Sometime. *By the end of the run, however, she said she had "learned not to blush."*

West was serenely unconcerned by what she considered jealousy on the part of her costars. "They soon discovered," she remarked later, "that I would not conform to the old-fashioned limits they had set on a woman's freedom of action. Or the myth of a woman's need of male wisdom and protection. This baffled them."

As World War I ended and the "Roaring Twenties" began, Mae West was more than ready to roar along with them. The rest of the world, it seemed, was coming closer to accepting her own philosophy of life.

West wears a flapper's version of Cleopatra's crown in the 1921 musical The Mimic World. *One mocking critic said her shimmy-dancing in this show "caught the true spirit of Egypt."*

FOUR

Playwright

The 1920s were years of almost desperate gaiety in the United States. Polka-dotted automobiles, bathtub gin, jazz music, and all-night dancing set the tone of the times. Women—who got the right to vote in 1920—began to "bob" their hair, shorten their skirts, use makeup, smoke cigarettes in public, and call themselves "flappers."

College students competed to see who could swallow the most live goldfish, daredevils vied for records in the sport of flagpole-sitting, and determined dancers plodded endlessly around brightly lit halls to win prizes in dance marathons.

It was in this "good-time" era that radio came of age. After station KDKA in Pittsburgh, Pennsylvania, broadcast the presidential election results in 1920 (Warren G. Harding defeated James Cox), thousands of Americans rushed to buy radios. The nation's vaudeville

houses began to transform themselves into glittering picture palaces as silent movies became the favorite entertainment of millions of Americans.

In 1919 the nation technically went "dry" when the 18th Amendment to the Constitution prohibited the sale of alcoholic beverages. Across the nation, "speakeasies" immediately sprang up by the dozens. They were especially thick in New York's theatrical center. Supplying these illegal but openly flourishing saloons were bootleggers—gangsters who smuggled liquor into the country and sold it to the millions of Americans to whom Prohibition was little more than a joke.

As well as selling alcoholic beverages to the "speaks," the bootleggers often frequented them, meeting and mingling with performers and theatergoers. On occasion, the Broadway-area saloons were the scene of shoot-outs

A 1925 flapper models the "in look" of the Jazz Age: lipstick, bobbed hair, cloche hat, and low-waisted, short-skirted dress. Such styles were revived in the 1980s.

A prospective customer knocks for admission to a "speakeasy," or illegal saloon, in the 1920s. Such drinking spots sprang up across the country after Prohibition was instituted in 1919.

between rival gangs of bootleggers. "Show business," as Mae West put it, "had a hard time trying to keep ahead of the headlines and still be entertaining."

In the midst of the country's frantic efforts to enjoy itself came the stern voices of restraint. After Prohibition came a movement toward censorship of the freewheeling entertainment industry.

Too many stage and screen perfor-

mances, thought some reform-minded observers, had become shockingly frank about sex, if not downright immoral. These reformers favored the immediate closing of any production they considered offensive. Their campaign for "decency" proved effective; not wanting to appear tolerant of "dirty" plays, civic officials were often ready to back up the reformers with police action.

In the early 1920s, the Producing

Radio station KDKA in Pittsburgh, Pennsylvania, set off what one historian called a "national mania" for the new medium when it broadcast the election results on November 2, 1920.

Managers' Association, an organization of theater owners, created a panel of reviewers to judge the moral acceptability of Broadway shows. The theater executives hoped that if the industry censored itself, the expensive embarrassment of police raids might be avoided.

Mae West continued to work on what was called the "legitimate" stage—Broadway, as opposed to vaudeville—through most of the 1920s. With the assistance of her new agent,

Jim Timony, she also began to write and produce full-length plays. She was buoyed in these efforts by Tillie West, who remained her daughter's most enthusiastic supporter.

"My mother was always behind me," said West in her autobiography, "pushing me, believing in me ever since I was little. She said, 'Dear, you always fix up all your characters so much that I know you can write your own play.'"

West picked a straightforward title for her first play: *Sex*. In the past, she pointed out, the word *sex* had only been used in such "unerotic" phrases as "the opposite sex" or "the fair sex." But times had changed, and now it was the name of a play, *her* play. "Biggest Sensation since the Armistice [the treaty that ended World War I]: Mae West in *Sex*," read the advertisement in *The New York Times* on the eve of the show's opening.

The starring role in *Sex* was that of Margie Lamont, a prostitute who—like all the characters West would create for herself—liked men, defied convention, and had a heart of gold. To stage the play, West, her mother, and Jim Timony had formed a corporation called The Moral Producing Company. As she often said of herself, West enjoyed a good joke.

The Producing Managers' Association had approved *Sex* as "clean," but the critics were not pleased. It was, said one reviewer, "a vulgar affair" that "relies on its sensationalism to cash in." The public, however, loved the play, which began to lure standing-room-only crowds as soon as it opened.

The success of her play was no mystery to West. "Everyone wants to write plays about a man and woman or men and men," she said. "But my style is a woman among men—just the reverse of what's always been written, see?" Theatergoers apparently did see—*Sex* ran for the next 30 weeks to packed houses.

Adding to the play's appeal was the campaign against it staged by two New York newspapers, the *Daily Mirror* and the *Graphic*. They ran frequent editorials condemning *Sex* as immoral and urging police action to shut it down. Far from being disturbed by the press attacks, West was delighted. "Every knock is a boost," she said. And she was right; piqued by the publicity, many people who did not ordinarily go to the theater bought tickets.

No policemen appeared to stop *Sex* from playing; it looked, in fact, as though it might go on for years. Wanting a new challenge, West began to use the time between performances to write a new play. This one was inspired by one of her admirers, a divorced man who confessed to being a bisexual.

West, who had always challenged convention, was stirred by his story. In her autobiography, she said she had felt "a strong compulsion to put down a realistic drama" about homosexuality, a "tragic" subject that was "met by ordinary people with a stare of shocked horror."

West said she had always gotten along well with the homosexuals with whom she worked in the theater, although she "had no personal emotional relations to the ideas of the theme." Never, she said, had she "had any private interest in a woman as a love object . . . yet here I was blithely writing a play that could only make trouble for me."

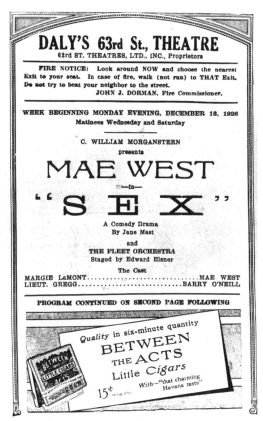

The controversial "comedy drama" Sex had already been running for eight months when this playbill was printed. "Jane Mast," listed as the play's author, was a pen name for Mae West.

James J. Walker talks to reporters in the late 1920s. The debonair New York City mayor had no objection to Sex, but his deputy, "Holy Joe" McKee, wanted it closed for immorality.

When West began to write that play, *The Drag*, she intended it to be a study of the pressures society brings to bear on unconventional people. This was a theme with which she could identify. Her talents, however, were not for social commentary. *The Drag* turned out to be less a statement about the persecution of homosexuals than a story of the sensational aspects of the homosexual life-style.

Just before the play was to begin its run on Broadway, it ran into trouble. John Sumner, spokesman for the Society for the Suppression of Vice, announced that if *The Drag* opened in Manhattan, he would insist on police action to close it. Not eager for a direct confrontation with the law, West and Jim Timony decided to cancel their plans to bring *The Drag* to Broadway.

Sumner may have been pleased by

43

After serving an eight-day prison term for "producing an immoral show" (Sex) in 1927, Mae West gets a hug from her mother, Tillie West. Looking on is Beverly West, the actress's sister.

his success in keeping *The Drag* out of New York, but he was not satisfied. He now turned his energies to West's long-running hit, *Sex*. James J. Walker, New York's easygoing and sophisticated mayor, had resisted reformers' demands that he prosecute the city's more uninhibited productions for "immorality." In February 1927, however, the mayor left for a vacation, leaving the city in charge of Acting Mayor Joseph McKee.

McKee, who was known as "Holy Joe," seized the chance to clean up New York. He authorized a series of raids on productions that had been singled out as offensive; one of them, unsurprisingly, was *Sex*, then in its 42nd successful week.

Along with performers from two other raided shows, West and her fellow cast members were arrested and herded into a police wagon. By the time West, who was used to riding in a chauffeur-driven limousine, boarded the vehicle, all the seats were taken; fuming, she stood all the way to prison. After spending a night in jail, all the actors were released on bail. A few weeks later, West, Timony, and the rest of the *Sex* cast were indicted by a grand jury for "producing an immoral show and maintaining a public nuisance."

The play had been allowed to continue until the trial, which was scheduled for March 28. It was doing turnaway business—the raid had actually improved attendance—but West

closed it on March 21, citing her "exhaustion." The trial turned out to be as popular with the public as the play.

West appeared in court in different outfits—usually black satin dresses, furs, and elaborate hats—every day. She played to the crowd, staring at the ceiling in amazement when the prosecution called her play "corrupting to the morals of youth," and modestly looking at the floor when her attorney compared her play with *Hamlet* and the Bible.

Courtroom spectators were amused not only by West's antics, but by the testimony of the vice-squad policeman. This burly sergeant inadvertently provoked roars of laughter when, to illustrate his testimony about the play's offensive nature, he imitated West's slinky walk and exaggerated gestures.

Much to West and Timony's surprise, the jury, whose members had been laughing along with the spectators, returned a verdict of guilty. The prosecutor was jubilant. "This verdict," he told reporters, "vindicates the theory that dirty plays successfully can be prosecuted before juries."

"If anybody needs a dirty play," West shot back, "they ought to call [prosecutor] Wallace for suggestions! He brought our conviction." *Sex*, she added, "was a work of art," as well as "one of the cleanest shows in town." Nevertheless, she and Timony were sentenced to $500 fines and 10-day jail terms.

Costumed as "Diamond Lil," West holds a drink in one hand and a cigarette in the other. Offstage, the "world's wickedest woman" used neither alcohol nor tobacco.

West served eight days in prison, having earned two days off her sentence for good behavior. Characteristically, she turned what could have been an unpleasant experience into a public-relations bonanza. In one interview after another, she praised the warden for giving her a private room, allowing her to wear her own clothes, and taking her for automobile drives in the evenings. She even managed to get herself invited to a charity luncheon sponsored by women's groups interested in juvenile delinquency.

While she was in jail, West had started writing a new play. Entitled *The Wicked Age*, it was a jazz-accented drama about the dishonesty and cruelty that characterized many of the popular beauty contests of the day. It opened in New York in November 1927 to uniformly scathing critical notices. One reviewer called it "gross, disgusting, tiresome, utterly futile vulgarity, without a single excusing feature or reason for being." *The Wicked Age* closed after 19 performances.

Never discouraged by criticism or temporary setbacks, West immediately set to work polishing and casting another new play, *Diamond Lil*. This one—whose title echoed her mother's nickname, Champagne Til—was a comedy-melodrama set in the 1890s (West's favorite historical period). Its central character, played, of course, by its author, was a sexy, tough woman with a gentle heart (West's favorite role).

Diamond Lil was a spectacular hit and a milestone in Mae West's career. For the first time, the drama critics of New York's major newspapers took her seriously as an actress. Their reviews of *Lil* were like mirror-images of their savage verbal attacks on *The Wicked Age*.

"I wouldn't miss *Diamond Lil* if I were you," advised the theater critic of the fashionable *New Yorker* magazine.

Even the somber *New York Times* admitted that West was "a good actress."

The *Evening Telegram* summed up the establishment's newfound admiration for *Diamond Lil*'s star. "So regal is Miss West's manner," said the *Telegram* review, "so assured is her artistry, so devastating are her charms in the eyes of all red-blooded men, so blond, so beautiful, so buxom is she that she makes Miss Ethel Barrymore [a reigning queen of the stage] look like the late lamented [comedian] Mr. Bert Savoy."

The public enthusiastically agreed with the critics. It was suddenly not only respectable, but chic, to be seen in the company of the "world's wickedest woman," as West was often dubbed. The well-wishers who crowded into her theater dressing room included sportswriters, social leaders, intellectuals, prize fighters, politicans, stage and film stars. West was pleased to be recognized as a genuine star, but she was also puzzled.

Diamond Lil was, after all, not so very different from her previous efforts. It was peopled with gritty but good-hearted lowlife characters, and the morals of its central character were by no means conventionally "pure." In the title role, West swished her hips and huskily uttered lines like "I'm one of the finest women who ever walked the streets." West knew she had not changed. It must, she reasoned, be the rest of the world that had.

West was still insistent about her

right to express her sexuality as she saw fit. "I freely chose the kind of life I led," she wrote later, "because I was convinced that a woman has as much right as a man to live the way she does if she does no actual harm to society. I saw no indecency or perversion in the normal private habits of men and women." (Or, she might have added, in their portrayal on stage.)

After *Diamond Lil* had played for almost a year on Broadway, West decided to take it on a cross-country tour. The show proved as successful in other cities as it had been in New York. It was especially popular in Chicago, where West was billed as "the most talked about star in the world." The play opened to standing-room-only crowds in San Francisco, but business dropped off sharply toward the end of 1929.

"Wall Street Lays an Egg," read the famous October 1929 headline in *Variety*. The stock market had crashed, ending the boom years of the 1920s and marking the beginning of the catastrophic worldwide depression of the 1930s. Millions of Americans had been borrowing money to invest in the stock market; now many of the stocks they had indebted themselves to buy were worthless. Almost overnight, businesses, factories, and shops closed their doors; within a year the rate of unemployment in the United States reached the highest point in history.

The theater was as hard-hit as other sectors of the economy. With little money available, Americans began to hesitate about spending it on such luxuries as theater tickets. The stock-buying craze had not passed over the entertainment business, and many actresses and actors found themselves wiped out financially. West was not among them.

"I was free of the rising panic," she wrote later. "What money I had was in show business, and in my diamonds. I didn't invest in something I couldn't sit and watch." Nevertheless, West was concerned about the money worries of her friends.

What worried her far more was her mother's failing health. Tillie West, 56, had terminal liver cancer. She had kept that fact from her daughter Mae as long as she could, but West knew her mother was ill. Nevertheless, when she visited her, she saw the same cheerful, carefully dressed and made-up woman she had always known.

The rest of the family was amazed at Tillie West's ability to hide the severity of her condition from her elder daughter, but there was nothing Mae West's mother would not try to do for her favorite child. By early 1930, however, not even Tillie West could keep up the pretense.

West had brought *Diamond Lil* back to the East Coast and was performing in a New York City theater on the night of January 26, 1930. In the middle of the second act, she got word that her

An unemployed New Yorker sells apples on a city street during the 1930s. Such sights were common during the Great Depression, when more than 12 million Americans were out of work.

mother was dying. Jim Timony urged the distraught star to go to her mother's side at once, but West, unshakably true to the theater's motto—"the show must go on"—finished her performance before she went home.

Moments after she arrived, her mother died. West was shattered, but she refused to follow the advice of friends and close her show. She was back on stage the following night. Her mother's death, she said later, "was the greatest shock and deepest sorrow of my life. I went to pieces. It took me

three years to get over it—no, not to get over it, but to live with it."

To distract herself from her grief, West began to write a novel. Published in 1930, *The Constant Sinner* was the story of a love affair between a black man and a white woman. The book, said West, "made literary critics sit up and turn pale." It sold well, and the Shubert theatrical production company asked West to turn it into a play.

Segregation, firmly established in American society in the 1930s, was a fact of life in the theater as well. West's interracial theme was a daring one, but not even she could get away with casting a black actor opposite the white leading lady—played, of course, by herself. She did insist, however, on hiring a black actor to understudy the male lead, and on casting black actors and actresses in the supporting roles.

West believed that people should be judged on their own merits, and she considered the prohibition against the onstage mixing of the races absurd. After its New York run, *The Constant Sinner* was booked for engagements in Washington, D.C., and Chicago. West planned to have black understudy Lorenzo Tucker take over the lead after the play had opened in Chicago. The play, however, ran into trouble before she could carry out her scheme.

Many years later, Lorenzo Tucker talked about West, Washington, and *The Constant Sinner*. "You have to give her credit," he said. "Washington was

Waiting to enter Loew's State theater, moviegoers crowd a Manhattan sidewalk in the late 1920s. The film palace's marquee explains its novel attraction: an "all talking" program.

totally segregated at the time. It took nerve to offer a black-and-white love story. . . . The district attorney, a fellow named Rover, came to the theater and told Miss West it just wasn't going to happen in Washington, having blacks and whites on stage. Well, she was determined to have it done, and Rover said she couldn't continue. But she said, 'My play stays the way it is.' And she stuck to it, even though it meant a big loss."

The Shubert organization, already close to bankruptcy because of the economic depression that had swept the country, told West it would have to close the show unless she agreed to eliminate the scenes between blacks and whites. She flatly refused, and *The Constant Sinner* folded. "People now say that wasn't much," said Tucker. "But I believe we have to look at folks like her with raised eyes and give them credit for their contribution."

By 1931 the two arenas in which West had achieved success had diminished radically. The "legitimate" theater was in distress and vaudeville had been virtually wiped out by the advent of the motion picture. West began to think about movies and to wonder how they "could use my style and personality."

Aware that her sultry voice was an essential part of the Mae West Character, she had been uninterested in silent films. "Talkies," however, were another matter. The first film with sound—*The Jazz Singer*, starring Al Jolson—had opened in 1927, heralding the birth of a new era in entertainment. When West's agent brought her a movie offer after *The Constant Sinner*'s closing, she hesitated, but not for long.

As she put it in her autobiography, "Could I stay in New York with the Palace Theater losing $4,000 a week? Broadway was in real trouble. Of 152

Actor Walter Petrie reassures West in a scene from The Constant Sinner, *her 1931 play about a white woman's love for a black man. The drama's interracial theme was a daring one for the time.*

plays that season [1931], 121 folded. Maybe, I decided, I'd take a fling at Hollywood." On January 16, 1932, she boarded a train for the West Coast. There, she said, she would learn how to "make leaping snapshots talk."

51

West displays her legs in a standard Hollywood publicity shot. Convinced that "what you don't show is more interesting than what you do," she rarely posed for such "cheesecake" pictures.

FIVE

Hollywood Goddess

Surrounded by reporters when she arrived in Hollywood, Mae West introduced herself. "I'm not," announced the 39-year-old actress, "a little girl from a little town here to make good in a big town. I'm a big girl from a big town who's come to make good in a little town."

That "little town" was not so sure it was pleased to see her. Louella Parsons, one of the screen colony's most powerful columnists, wrote "The buxom blonde Mae West, fat, fair and I don't know how near 40, has come to Hollywood. It's a contract that the plumpish Miss West holds in her two fists. The contract is with Paramount and it calls for an important part...."

The part was in *Night After Night*, a gangster comedy that was to star George Raft. West and Raft had met during the New York production of *Diamond Lil* in 1928, and she had made

a deep impression on the gravel-voiced actor.

Paramount Pictures viewed Raft as the natural successor to Rudolph Valentino, the "Great Lover" of the silent screen who had died in 1926. As a star, Raft was allowed to help cast his own films; for *Night After Night*, he had asked for Mae West.

At first West was unsure about her future in Hollywood. In her autobiography she recalled wondering, "Would I make it in a land of palm trees, restaurants shaped like derby hats, goose-fleshed bathing beauties, and far-flung custard pies? Could I show my stuff in the city of oranges, Warner Brothers, and swimming pools? I had no doubt about my talents, but I was aware I faced a barrier."

West knew that few Hollywood people had much respect for the abilities of stage and vaudeville perform-

George Raft, who had once worked for New York bootlegger Owney Madden, was hired by Paramount Pictures to play gangster roles. The studio, however, soon began to cast him as a romantic hero.

Fans mob a theater playing The Sheik, Rudolph Valentino's 1921 blockbuster silent film. The 31-year-old matinee idol's sudden death in 1926 plunged millions of women into mourning.

ers. She knew she would face strong opposition if she tried to impose her own hard-won theatrical expertise on the making of a film. She had, however, every intention of doing just that.

She settled into an apartment near the Paramount studios and waited impatiently for her movie script. When reporters showed up to interview her, she cheerfully reinforced her "wicked" image. "I'm here to make talkies," she said. "I hope the film can take the temperature." She was delighted with her apartment, which she began to redecorate in white and gold.

When West finally read the script for

Night After Night, she was furious. Maudie Triplett, the character she was to play, did not appear until the movie was half over. To make matters worse, Maudie was dull, humorless, and of minor importance in the plot.

West stormed into the office of the studio chief. Her "personality," she said, would be "wasted" in the role, one that could easily be played by "any doll under contract." Reminded that *she* was under contract, West drew herself up to her full five feet and informed the astounded Hollywood executives that she wanted to return "all the lovely money that has been paid me" and go back to New York.

The film's producer, William Le Baron, had written the book for *A La*

West gives an interview in the Hollywood apartment where she lived from 1932 until 1980. Decorated in white, gold, and pink, it boasted three polar bear rugs and dozens of mirrors.

Broadway, the 1911 show in which West had written much of her own musical material. He remembered that she had a gift for amusing dialogue. When he heard about her threat to leave the picture, he told her to rewrite the part of Maudie Triplett, adding whatever "Westian" lines she wanted.

West immediately withdrew her resignation and set to work on the script. "I entirely rewrote my part and gave myself my best-styled dialogue," she said later. "What was good for me," she added with typically Westian reason-

ing, "was good for the picture." When she finished, she had created just what she wanted—what one observer called "a lady of no character."

West arrived on the sound stage with rewritten scenes, her own diamonds and furs, and a determination to re-create the Mae West Character on film. "It was her first screen appearance," George Raft said later, "and her cleverness on the stage was a new kind of thievery to me. She stole everything but the cameras." Alison Skipworth, the veteran actress who appeared in several scenes with West, knew what Raft meant.

West, complained Skipworth, was deliberately upstaging her, stealing her best scenes. At last she turned to the upstart blond from New York and said icily, "You forget I've been an actress for 40 years." West smiled sweetly. "Don't worry, dear," she said, "I'll keep your secret."

Night After Night opened in October 1932. It was a smash hit, thanks in large part to West and the lines she had con-tributed to the script. In one scene, she knocks at the door of a private club. Asked by the doorman to identify herself, she says, "The fairy princess, you mug!" She sweeps past him, revealing her glittering jewelry as she tosses her furs to the hatcheck attendant. The next lines made screen history.

Hatcheck woman, dazzled: "Goodness, what beautiful diamonds!"

West, sultry-voiced: "Goodness had nothing to do with it, dearie."

Despite the huge box-office receipts

Ignoring Alison Skipworth's scowl and George Raft's puzzled expression, West smilingly proposes a champagne toast in a scene from her first movie, 1932's Night After Night.

for *Night After Night*, Paramount executives hesitated about signing West for another picture. The studio's financial picture was bleak—the company had recorded an $18 million profit in 1930 and a $21 million loss in 1932—and the executives were worried about West's future with the censors.

Hollywood had instituted its own system of self-censorship in 1922. It was administered by the president of the Motion Picture Producers and Distributors of America, Will Hays. Like Broadway's Producing Managers' Association, the Hays Office, as the board came to be called, tried to anticipate censorship problems before films were released.

Nevertheless, various self-appointed guardians of public morality were becoming increasingly vocal in their opposition to suggestiveness in movies. The management of Paramount suspected that if West made another picture, she might overstep the bounds set by such organizations as the National Legion of Decency.

While the studio was hesitating, the public was demonstrating its own sentiments. The Paramount mailroom was suddenly flooded with fan mail for West, and 5,500 movie-theater owners rebooked *Night After Night*.

"They weren't sure what they had," Bill Thomas, the publicity man who had been hired to promote West, observed later. "Hollywood didn't think she was any big thing. She was just set

Mae West responds to the line, "Goodness, what beautiful diamonds!" with the words that launched her movie career: "Goodness had nothing to do with it, dearie."

for two or three scenes in Raft's picture. But neither I nor anybody else suspected that Mae was going to rescue the studio [from bankruptcy]. I mean, who could know?"

By now everybody knew. Paramount scheduled the immediate production of *She Done Him Wrong*, the new title for West's old hit play, *Diamond Lil*. West often told the story of how she selected the leading man for her new movie. She had looked at photographs of all the studio's male stars, and found none that suited her. On her way out of the casting office with Paramount executive Al Kaufman, she saw "a sensational-looking young man."

West said she wanted *him* for her

leading man. Kaufman objected, explaining that the young actor had so far appeared only in screen tests. "Call him over," said West. "If he can talk, I'll take him." He was introduced, spoke in a "charming accent," and got the job. His name was Cary Grant.

The first writer assigned to *She Done Him Wrong* was a New Yorker named John Bright. He considered West a gifted and highly professional actress. "There has never been a stage constructed," he said, "that she couldn't dominate." He did not, however, have a high opinion of West's writing ability.

Bright had seen the stage version of *Diamond Lil*, which he had thought "funny" only because it was "so terrible." West, he said, might "be a great personality, a unique personality, but she can't spell 'cat.' She knows nothing of construction. She couldn't hold down a job on a radio soap opera."

When Bright took on the job of writing *She Done Him Wrong*, he assumed that West would do what she did best—act—and leave the script to him. He was very much mistaken. West considered herself a skilled playwright, and she grew more and more annoyed by Bright's lack of admiration for her contributions to the screenplay.

Finally, West told producer Le Baron that either she or Bright would have to leave the picture. Bright left. He had already written most of the screenplay, but he wound up sharing the writing credit with a "housebroken" writer

In She Done Him Wrong, *the film version of West's beloved* Diamond Lil, *tough but goodhearted Lady Lou (West) is menaced by beautiful but evil Russian Rita (Rafaela Ottiano).*

who was more tactful in his dealings with West. "Most stars," said the rueful Bright afterward, "despite all their arrogance, are quite humble before writers because they do realize they need us badly. But not West."

Meanwhile, *She Done Him Wrong* was under close scrutiny by the Hays Office. Hays's Hollywood representative, Joseph Breen, finally announced that the movie could be made, but with certain restrictions. "In view of the low tone of backgrounds and characters," said Breen, "comedy should be em-

West flashes her diamonds in a publicity shot for She Done Him Wrong. *Before studio executives settled on the film's final title, they had considered* Diamond Lady, Honkey Tonk, *and* Ruby Red.

West identifies her own mannequin — a "perfect 36" — in the Paramount wardrobe department. Her lavish screen costumes were often designed by Edith Head, winner of eight Academy Awards.

phasized." This presented no problem for West; comedy, parody, and self-parody had been her specialties for two decades.

Breen also demanded 25 specific changes in script, action, costume, and song. West, for example, was forbidden to change her dress behind a screen in the movie. By today's standards, even the uncensored *She Done Him Wrong* would probably rate a PG-13 rat-

ing, but Americans were more easily shocked in the 1930s.

Despite the movie's basically innocent content and the Hays Office's efforts, several countries refused to allow its distribution, and a number of others cut it radically. Surprisingly, it caused few complaints in the sometimes puritanical United States. It turned out to be as popular in small towns as in big cities, which West found perfectly natural. People everywhere, she said, were "fascinated with sin."

At one point in *She Done Him Wrong*, Lady Lou, as played by West, meets a Salvation Army captain and says, "Why don't you come up sometime and see me? I'll tell your fortune." Many moviegoers remember the line as "Come up and see me sometime," but West did not say that until her next film, *I'm No Angel*. In any case, the line is pure Mae West, and entirely in keeping with her definition of the Mae West Character.

West always tried to explain to writers that it was that character that her fans paid to see. When they look at the screen, she said, they see not the heroine of the movie, "they see Mae West. And they'll hold it against her if she does or says something they don't like."

West went so far as to draw up a code of conduct for the Mae West Character. She gave it to all her writers and insisted that they follow it exactly. These were the rules: "Mae West can never take another woman's husband, chase a man, play a mother, expose her limbs, or be pushed around by another character. Mae West must always handle every situation with queenly grace, emerge totally triumphant from every encounter, and make the audience laugh."

In her early days in Hollywood, West had trouble getting used to the team effort required in moviemaking. Here,

collaboration among star, crew members, director, and writer was more important than it was on Broadway. West's co-workers found her difficult at first. They did not understand that she was a perfectionist, and that work was the central force in her life.

West was unlike the other "goddesses" of the screen: she did not smoke, did not drink, did not really care what people thought of her as long as they respected her work. Eventually, however, she established a reputation as a dedicated professional and earned the admiration of the Hollywood establishment.

Cary Grant, West's costar in *She Done Him Wrong*, was impressed with the speed with which she learned the differences between stage and film acting techniques. "She instinctively knew everything about camera angles and lighting," he wrote later, "and she taught me all I know about timing." Like all West's leading men, Grant projected a suave and gentlemanly personality, the perfect foil for West's earthy humor. After their successful partnership in *She Done Him Wrong*, the two became lifelong friends.

Before the film had begun shooting, West had told studio executives she wanted a week to rehearse with the cast. This would have been standard practice on Broadway, but it was unheard of in Hollywood. The executives told West that it would be much too expensive to pay for a week's rehearsal on top of paying for the 15 to 20 weeks it would take to shoot the elaborate costume movie.

West said, "I think *She Done Him Wrong* can be done in three weeks." The meeting room was suddenly silent. "First," she recalled, "came their puzzled expressions, then a smile of doubt and a sly look from one head to the other. I could read their minds transmitting, 'We know it can't be done, don't we?'"

West got her rehearsal time and the studio got its picture in 18 days. *She Done Him Wrong* was released in January 1933 and went on to become the top box-office film of the year. Mae West had saved Paramount Pictures from bankruptcy.

Movie critics were much impressed with West's portrayal of "the screen's first lady gangster." In most Hollywood pictures of the time, outlaws were idealized, then killed in the last reel to prove that "justice always triumphs." West, on the other hand, had played Lady Lou as a real woman who had the strength and courage to change her life.

After the film's release, publicity man Bill Thomas arranged a deal with the manufacturer of Old Gold cigarettes. The company would advertise the film along with its own product, and West would endorse the cigarettes for a payment of $1500. The promotion scheme delighted eveybody but West. She did not smoke, she said, and she would not endorse a tobacco product.

Paramount told Thomas to change West's mind if he was interested in his future with the company. He went to West and told her how important the deal was to him. "So it means a lot, huh?" Thomas later recalled her asking. He assured her that it did, and she quickly signed the contract.

Then, reported Thomas, West said, "You keep the fifteen hundred. But don't go around telling everybody. They'll think I'm a soft touch, see?" That, said Thomas, "was the kind of dame she was."

Although West cherished her hard-as-nails image, she was indeed a "soft touch." Like many famous people, she was bombarded by requests for money; old vaudeville friends who were down on their luck, rising young performers who needed a boost, religious, charitable, and professional organizations were among the numerous individuals and groups that sought her help. She often gave it, her one condition being secrecy.

At one point, a reporter asked her to confirm a story that she had given $25,000 to the Motion Picture Relief Fund. "It's true," she snapped, "but you can't print it." She once said that it "depressed" her "to see nuns riding on buses." When she decided she needed a new limousine, the one she had been using always went to a con-

Enthroned in her movie-queen-sized bed, West chats with her sister Beverly. Although some wags compared her apartment to a "French candy box," West was immensely proud of it.

vent. She also had intense sympathy for the young, particularly for youthful, unwed mothers, and she quietly funneled thousands of dollars to organizations that cared for them.

Within two years of her arrival in Hollywood, West had become known as America's new "sex goddess." Little affected by her increased celebrity, she continued to enjoy such favorite pastimes as attending boxing and wrestling matches with her friend and agent Jim Timony. She also kept up with her old friends in New York, finding jobs in Hollywood for many of them.

During a New York promotion tour for *She Done Him Wrong*, West went to a restaurant in Harlem for dinner. There she ran into Libby Taylor, an old friend. Taylor, a black actress West had known in her vaudeville days, was working as a cook in the restaurant. Needing a "straight woman" (a partner in a comic act) for her tour, West signed her on. The two worked well together. When West returned to Hollywood, she brought Taylor, whom she featured in the next two movies she made.

Taylor was the first of several black actresses to play West's maid on screen. (Another was Hattie McDaniel, who later became famous in *Gone with the Wind*.) Phyllis Klotman of the University of Indiana's Afro-American Studies Department recently commented on West's relationships with these women:

"Although in subservient positions and acting often as foils for Mae West's barbed one-liners ('It's not the men in your life, it's the life in your men!'), they were more ... confidantes than typical mammy maids.... Not a great deal was made of it, but Mae's conversations with her confidantes indicate that

Cary Grant and Mae West exchange a romantic look in I'm No Angel, *their second film together. "Those two pictures," said Grant later, "gave me the kind of showcase every actor dreams of."*

current male friends, and when they did, they rushed into print. Far from being distressed by West's notoriety, studio executives considered it good for business. It seemed that the more her fans read about West, the more letters they wrote her and the more theater tickets they bought.

After the success of *She Done Him Wrong*, Paramount was eager to find another good script for West. One day, she told a writer friend that if she had not succeeded as an actress, she might have become a lion tamer. From there, it was a short step to creating a script about a woman who worked with big cats in the circus.

Entitled *I'm No Angel*, the film went into production in July 1933. To prepare for her role, West studied the techniques used by Mabel Stark, a Los Angeles animal trainer who specialized in wrestling tigers. Stark had scars all over her body from her years of work with jungle animals, but West envied her. She told the trainer that if she had to be anyone but herself, she would be Mabel Stark. "We'll switch," replied Stark. "I wish I were Mae West."

One of the film's most memorable scenes shows the heroine placing her head in a lion's mouth. Following standard Hollywood practice, the director prepared to shoot the scene with a stunt woman, but West balked. "This lion scene," she said, "is the main reason I'm doing this picture." Studio ex-

these women do have a life of their own."

West was unlike the typical Hollywood star of her time in many ways. Most members of the screen's "royalty" were disdainful of their fans, but West loved them and she showed it. "The legitimate theater had taught me," she said, "that the success of a star depends upon a continuous love affair between her and her audience." She did try to keep her personal relationships secret from Hollywood's ever-present gossip columnists, but here she had little success.

One way or another, the columnists usually learned the identity of West's

Cuddling up to one of her costars in I'm No Angel, *West raises a triumphant salute; despite her director's objections, she had just succeeded in placing her head in the lion's mouth.*

ecutives raced to the set and explained that what she wanted was impossible.

They said, West recalled, that "aside from the humanitarian feeling of not wanting to have me mangled or killed, the business risk of losing both me and the picture was not to be taken lightly." West was not be taken lightly, either. As one of the actors in the movie put it, "There was a real sweetness about

West strikes an unusually pensive pose in a mid-1930s portrait. After I'm No Angel *broke box-office records, she began to think of herself as a "prisoner" of her own success.*

her. But you'd no more think of crossing her than you would an army drill sergeant." In the end, West played the scene without a double.

Gorgeously costumed in an ermine cape and a white and gold military outfit, she entered the lions' cage, cracked her whip, and put the animals through their paces. Finally, she approached the largest lion and pried open its mouth. A tense silence descended on the set as she put her head between its jaws. The lion behaved like a trou-

per, the cameras recorded the scene, and the director yelled, "Cut!" Beaming and unscratched, West emerged from the cage to the cheers of the crew.

Unknown to West, the cage had been ringed with sharpshooters instructed to kill any animal that menaced her. "I was confident that I would be safe," she remarked afterward, "but apparently no one else was."

When the lion-tamer movie opened in October 1933, it evoked a roar of approval from critics and public alike. It broke box-office records across the country and received surprisingly serious reviews from what West referred to as "the large-head set."

Critic William Troy of *The Nation* magazine, for example, said the movie had "a great deal of interest, although of an oblique and rather intellectual nature." West's acting style, he said, was both "in the tradition of American burlesque" and a "burlesque of that tradition."

"Whatever one may think of that tradition," Troy continued, "it must be granted that Miss West has brought it to its classic culmination. . . . So perfectly does she now sum up in her own person—her speech, gestures, and carriage—the main elements of her tradition that she no longer requires a story or even a backdrop. She would be effective on a bare concert stage."

Many of today's serious film students consider *I'm No Angel*—which once again featured Cary Grant as West's main love interest—West's finest movie. In a recent book, *The Films of Mae West*, author Jon Tuska discusses the "moral philosophy" of the picture, which, he says, "has to do with the admission of woman's sexual nature, no less legitimate than a man's."

The character West plays, says Tuska, "embraces all of life and all of man, without hatred or pettiness, but with wit, tolerance, equality, and with personal capability, mastery of herself and her world, the world in which she lives and, by extension, the world in which all of us must live."

When West made *I'm No Angel*, she was 40 years old, outlandishly ancient by the Hollywood standards of the 1930s. Nevertheless, her earthy appeal as Tira, the sensual lion tamer, was unquestionable. Under the headline, "West Scorches Paramount Screen," a New York newspaper reported, "The West heat wave is rapidly spreading over the entire country."

West's movies are still celebrated for their sly quips, and *I'm No Angel* had a fine selection. Millions of moviegoers enjoyed such lines as, "When I'm good, I'm very good, but when I'm bad, I'm better." While there were the usual complaints about "vulgarity" and "crudeness," the film made more than $3 million, at least six times the amount then regarded as a highly successful return. West summed up the phenomenon in typical fashion. "Virtue has its own reward," she said, "but not at the box office."

The Hays Office, however, did reward "virtue," and it saw little of it in Mae West's movies. After the release of *I'm No Angel*, the censors became more zealous than ever in their scrutiny of film scripts. Because West was now one of Hollywood's most powerful and independent-minded stars, Hays and his staff paid special attention to her material. "I soon saw," she said in her autobiography, that "I was a prisoner of my publicity and my success."

Playing Ruby Carter, "Queen of the entertainers from St. Louis," West belts out a torch song in the 1934 movie Belle of the Nineties. *The score included "Memphis Blues" and "My Old Flame."*

SIX

Troubled Waters

The Hays Office decided that with *I'm No Angel*, Mae West had scorched her last screen. Citizens' organizations and religious groups were campaigning for tighter controls; Hollywood's censors knew that if they did not "clean up" the movie industry themselves, the studios would be saddled with ironclad legal censorship.

The Hays Office's rules for subjects that movies could and could not depict grew increasingly complex. Double beds were strictly forbidden, even in films with married characters. Interracial marriages were out, and crime could never be shown in detail. Wrongdoers had to die at the end of the movie unless it was clear that they had repented and reformed. Any suggestion of sex and/or passion was strongly discouraged.

The new codes verged on the absurd; a ruling prohibiting exposure of the reproductive organs, for example, applied even to the apes in the popular "Tarzan" movies. The simian performers were obliged to wear body stockings on screen.

West's 1934 film, *Belle of the Nineties*, was among the first movies to feel the weight of the reinforced "decency" rules. Although the finished picture contained a full measure of "Westisms"—"It's better to be looked over than overlooked"; "A man in the house is worth two on the street"—its overall content had been carefully sanitized by the Hays Office. The censor, reported West, "was on the set every day, enjoying himself."

Backed by the great Duke Ellington orchestra, West sang several numbers in *Belle of the Nineties*, including "My Old Flame" and "Troubled Waters," a jazz-flavored spiritual. The censors considered even the songs suggestive

Duke Ellington (center) and his orchestra were important to Belle of the Nineties. *Paramount executives had wanted to use recorded music for the film, but West insisted on the real thing.*

and required frequent retakes of the musical scenes.

Tongue in cheek, West once confessed that she "always found it a good policy to slip a few items into a script that the censors would cut out. It gave them a sense of accomplishing their job, and they were also less likely to cut out the things I really wanted to keep in."

West may have joked about the restraints imposed on her, but she was not happy about them. In her autobiography, she wrote, "I resented a type of censorship that quibbled over every line as if a devil were hiding behind each word."

That, in fact, was the problem: no matter how much her lines had been revised, when West delivered them,

they sounded "dirty" to some people. As she had said to reporters during her first censorship battle, more than 20 years earlier, "It wasn't what I said, but how I said it."

West's fans were loyal, and despite *Belle of the Nineties'* "purification," they flocked to see it. "A whitewashed Mae West," said a spokesman for Chicago's Apollo Theater, "is still able to pack them in." Of the print of *Belle* that he had seen, one critic wrote, "Best of the censored versions. Yes, in spite of all the interference, Mae West has given us a grand picture—almost as good as *She Done Him Wrong.* With good taste and laughs aplenty, Mae . . . will have you in the aisles."

West's popularity continued to rise, and so did her income. Under a new contract negotiated by Jim Timony, she earned $334,000 in 1934 and $480,000 the following year. Real estate had always interested her, and now she began to look for California property to buy. She had a good eye for value. One of her first purchases was a parcel of land in what later became the thriving city of Van Nuys. She paid $16,000 for it; by the 1970s, it would be worth more than $5 million.

West invited her father, who was in failing health, and her sister and brother-in-law to come and live on the 16-acre orange ranch she bought in 1934. She was pleased to have her family near her and glad to make peace with her 72-year-old father. "Battling Jack" West died a year after his arrival in California. Mae West would never forget the kindness of Jim Timony, who devoted much time to her father during his last months.

West's quiet, hardworking existence during these years was a far cry from the wild life that the studio publicity department claimed she led. She knew that colorful press releases were good for her image, and she went along with the publicists' flights of fancy. Sometimes, however, she felt they went too far in their promotional efforts.

When she learned that a number of manufacturers had been given permission to use her photograph and signature to advertise their products, she put her foot down. She dispatched a memo to the studio saying, "Will restrain anyone, legally, if they attach my name to a corset or gas station." Nevertheless, the Mae West Character—referred to even by West as a separate individual—had a life of its own.

People all over America had begun to quote West's one-liners, and "Mae West jokes," as their subject put it, "ran like greyhounds all over the land." Traditional "traveling salesman" and "farmer's daughter" jokes, she noted with delight, "were revamped to give them a Mae West twist."

West's success led to a rash of professional look-alikes. Recognizing a trend when they saw one, the heads

West, who loved diamonds, displays some favorites during an interview. Asked how she had acquired so much jewelry, she quoted one of her mottos: "Keep cool and collect."

of other Hollywood film studios began to develop their own versions of Paramount's West. Actresses known for their cultivated manner were instructed to sway when they walked and to speak in sultry tones. One studio, which specialized in making movies for black audiences, promoted an elaborately gowned and bejewelled

Flanked by a pair of Hollywood starlets, West exhibits a handbag topped with her initials. Posing for such publicity photographs was all in a day's work for the era's stars.

star whom they billed as the "Sepia Mae West."

The "Mae West look" became fashionable with American women of all social classes. Newspapers and magazines credited West with bringing back curves and inspiring a fad for diamonds, jeweled shoe buckles, and other extremely feminine styles of the 1890s, her favorite historical period.

Never one to underrate her own achievements, West wrote, "I had created a kind of 20th-century sex goddess that mocked and delighted all victims and soldiers of the great war between men and women. I was their banner, their figurehead, an articulate image, and I certainly enjoyed the work."

West may have been adored by her fans, but she was not popular among Hollywood's social elite. She had become good friends with Kitty Stromberg, the wife of well-known producer Hunt Stromberg, but theirs was one of the few Hollywood mansions where West was welcomed. Years later, the Strombergs' son explained why West had been snubbed by the film community's upper class: "It was rumored," he said, that "she hung around with blacks, wrestlers, and fags."

Always self-confident and independent, West was not even slightly concerned about her rejection by Hollywood society. She did indeed count a number of blacks, fighters, and homosexuals among her friends, and she was fiercely loyal to all of them. A reader can easily imagine the language she might have used if she had been advised to drop them in order to become socially "acceptable."

"The studio demanded I keep making pictures and I saw no reason to stop," wrote West about the mid-1930s. The 1935 movie *Goin' to Town* tells the story of a woman who discovers that her hardworking engineer sweetheart is really an English lord. Paramount insisted that West self-censor her script before it was submitted to the Hays Office. They wanted no repeat of the costly retakes the censors had required during the shooting of *Belle of the Nineties*.

High-society gamblers gape as Cleo Bordon (West) rakes in the chips in 1935's Goin' to Town. *Much more sedate than West's earlier films, this one received only lukewarm reviews.*

West reluctantly complied; it was obvious that if she wanted to continue to make movies, she had little choice. But the situation infuriated her. "Every person who is not a moron or a mental defective of some sort," she said in her autobiography, "carries a very effective censor and super-critic of his actions in his cerebral cortex—and in his heart. If that doesn't work, no amount of censorship from outside will do anybody any good."

When *Goin' to Town* was released, film critics were divided in their ap-praisals of West's uncharacteristically prim film. A brisk box-office business was assured, however, by a scandal that hit the press in April 1935. A Milwaukee office worker had accidentally uncovered a dusty marriage license; dated 1911, it was signed by Frank Wallace and Mae West. Newspaper reporters quickly latched onto the discovery.

West had always told interviewers that she had never been married. Questioned about the Milwaukee license, she continued to insist she was no

73

Frank Wallace, who had secretly married West in 1911, holds hands with his vaudeville partner, Trixie LeMay, in 1935. After the marriage was revealed, Wallace billed himself as "Mr. Mae West."

West talks with her lawyer before testifying in court about her marriage to Frank Wallace. She repeatedly denied that the wedding had taken place, but under oath, she finally admitted the truth.

man's wife. "Frank Wallace?" she asked. "Why, I never heard of the guy."

Reporters located ex-vaudevillian Wallace, now unemployed. Yes, he said, he had married Mae West in 1911, and yes, he was still married to her. The press interviewed most of West's friends and associates, along with anyone who might have known her and Wallace in 1911. Since few people had been aware of the marriage at the time, most of those questioned confirmed West's version of the story.

Nevertheless, the license application indicated that the bride had been born in Brooklyn in 1893, and that her parents were named John and Matilda. Hoping to win a large cash settlement, Wallace finally hired a lawyer. Complicated legal maneuvers kept the case out of court for two years; in the meantime, Wallace began to appear in nightclubs, billing himself as "Mr. Mae West."

When Wallace's lawsuit was heard in court in July 1937, West had to testify under oath. At last she admitted that she had married Wallace, but she said

"The Frisco Doll" (West) visits a miner's shack in Klondike Annie. *Publisher William Randolph Hearst labeled the 1936 film "filthy," but it was one of the actress's tamer efforts.*

the two had never lived together as man and wife. The case remained unresolved, bouncing in and out of court for the next five years.

In 1942 Wallace brought a new suit, this time asking for a million-dollar settlement plus a permanent monthly income of $1,000. West countersued, filed for a divorce, and received it. "Rumors had it," she wrote later, "that in the end I felt a little sorry for Frank and made him a settlement. He did get a few blue chips [stocks] as a present from me."

In 1936 West was once again hot news, this time for two reasons. The first was the release of her new film, *Klondike Annie*, in which she played a cabaret singer who, falsely accused of murder, poses as a missionary and flees to Alaska. The film contained several effective musical numbers, including a showstopper called "I'm an Occidental Woman in an Oriental Mood for Love."

Publisher William Randolph Hearst escorts actress Marion Davies to a 1942 military ball. Despite his long-term extramarital affair with Davies, Hearst condemned Mae West for "immorality."

The second cause of West's 1936 prominence was a furious press campaign against her. It was staged by powerful publisher William Randolph Hearst, owner of a chain of newspapers that reached across the United States.

Although Hearst was married, he had more or less publicly kept a minor movie star, Marion Davies, as his mistress for many years. His public posture, however, was that of a staunch defender of "female purity" and of the "sacred institution of the American family." After the release of *Klondike Annie*, Hearst claimed that both were threatened by Mae West.

By the time *Klondike Annie* was re-leased, it had been relentlessly scrubbed by the Hays Office. Among the written "recommendations" Hays officials had sent to Paramount had been these: Doll (the dance-hall queen who masquerades as a missionary, played by West) should be shown "playing games, possibly with rough miners, teaching them Mother Goose rhymes, etc." Doll should also teach the "rough miners" to "cut out paper dolls or play charades."

Determined to make Doll a role model for young women, the Hays Office urged that at the end of the movie, she should be shown "spending her money freely for some good purpose, say the hiring of an airplane to get serum for a dying child." (The fact that the movie was set in 1900—before the first successful flight—seems not to have crossed the censors' minds.)

No matter how "clean" the Hays Office had made the movie, Hearst wanted it and its star stopped. In a memo to the editors of all his news-papers, he said, "The Mae West picture, *Klondike Annie*, is a filthy picture.... It is an affront to the decency of the public and to the interests of the motion picture profession.

"Will Hays must be asleep to allow such a thing to come out, but it is to be hoped the churches of the community are awake to the necessity of boycotting such a picture and demanding its prompt withdrawal. After you have had a couple of good editorials regarding the indecency of this picture then *do not mention Mae West in our papers again . . . and do not accept any advertising for this picture.*"

West had spent much of her life battling the kind of hypocrisy that Hearst represented, but Hearst himself was too powerful to fight. His campaign compounded her problems with the censors and made Paramount begin to think of her as a liability. Other leading performers were nervous about ap-

Henry Hathaway, director of Go West, Young Man, *was known as a tough man, but he was no match for Mae West. "Power," he said of the actress. "That's what interested her."*

pearing in West's films; sharing the screen with such a notorious actress might, they thought, hurt their careers.

When her contract with Paramount expired in 1936, West moved over to Major Pictures, an independent company owned by former Paramount producer Emanuel Cohen. As soon as he had signed West, Cohen hired Henry Hathaway to direct her in a film called *Go West, Young Man*. Its main character was a movie star who falls in love with a handsome farmer after her limousine breaks down in a small town.

Hathaway, who had directed such recent smash hits as *Lives of a Bengal Lancer*, had a reputation for being tough on actors. That was before he met Mae West. "She called the shots—all of them," he said later. When, for example, he filmed a scene where the laugh would have come from the way West's dog walked, she ordered it cut. "Nobody," she declared, "gets laughs on my pictures but me."

Randolph Scott, the picture's male lead, was unusually tall. West was not, and she hated the idea of looking up to a costar. She insisted that Hathaway film her apart from Scott whenever it was possible. When the two played close-up scenes, Hathaway suggested that West stand on a box, but she said it would be uncomfortable. The close-ups were shot with Scott standing in a hole.

Once he got used to working with

West, Hathaway was philosophical. "Look," he said to producer Cohen, "none of her films are very good—unless you like Mae West. If you do, they're wonderful. Mae is the picture, and we focus it around her. Hell, any director who works with her is working with a woman who is completely special."

West's next film for Cohen was *Every Day's a Holiday*, which featured jazz-man Louis Armstrong and his orchestra. West played a blond adventuress from New York who returns from a trip to Paris wearing a black wig and claiming to be a popular French singer. West called her character "Peaches," which, she said, "the boys back in Brooklyn used to call me when I was a kid."

West had taken great pains to eliminate anything that might be considered offensive from the movie's script,

Randolph Scott shows Mae West a new machine in Go West, Young Man. *The 1936 comedy was one of the few films in which West, who loved the styles of the 1890s, wore contemporary clothing.*

but Hays Office officials said they would rate it "adults only" unless she agreed to remove two lines. The lines seemed perfectly innocent to West, but neither she nor Cohen wanted to lose their young audiences, and she agreed to the cuts. When *Every Day's a Holiday* was released, one reviewer summed up the general reaction. It was, he said, "scrupulously clean but funny."

West did not consider this assessment of her work a compliment. When she had come to Hollywood, she had intended to bring the Mae West Character to the screen exactly as she had created it. Yet by now, five years later, she was censoring her own work so thoroughly that it was being approved by the Hays Office with very few changes.

"I've never believed in going haywire on stage or screen," she said in her autobiography. "Obviously no medium of mass entertainment can be allowed to throw all restraint out the window. Strict censorship, however, has a reverse effect. It creates resentment on the part of the public. They feel that their freedom of choice is being dictated."

In late 1937 West was offered an irresistible opportunity to dodge the censors: she was invited to be a guest star on the Edgar Bergen–Charlie McCarthy radio show. In the days before television, radio—along with movies—was the nation's favorite form of entertainment. The Bergen-McCarthy show, officially known as the "Chase and Sanborn Hour" (because it was sponsored by the coffee manufacturer), had just been voted the most popular in America.

The script for the program called for West to have a fast-paced opening exchange with ventriloquist Bergen and his wisecracking dummy, Charlie McCarthy. Then she was to take part in a comedy skit about the Garden of Eden. Adam would be played by the well-known actor, Don Ameche; Charlie would be the serpent and Eve, of course, would be played by Mae West.

During rehearsals, West delivered her lines as written, but once she was on the air (radio shows were almost always performed live), she cut loose, adding typical Westian touches. She "reminded" Charlie about his visit to her apartment where, she said, "you didn't need any encouragement to kiss me." Going along with the gag, Bergen had the wooden dummy respond, "Did I do that?" West adopted her most sultry voice. "You certainly did. I got the marks to prove it—and the splinters, too."

Such dialogue would raise no eyebrows today, but radio in the 1930s reflected the extremely conservative attitudes of small-town America, and the West-McCarthy repartee bordered on the risqué. The Garden of Eden sketch followed; because it dealt hu-

Ventriloquist Edgar Bergen covers his face in mock horror as his dummy, Charlie McCarthy, swaps racy wisecracks with West. The exchange took place on radio's "Chase and Sanborn Hour" in 1937.

morously with a Bible story, it, too, was somewhat daring for the times, but the studio audience laughed loudly at West's slinky portrayal of Eve.

The next day, no one connected with the show was laughing. Newspapers began to receive letters expressing listeners' shocked reactions to the broadcast. It was called "obscene," "filthy," and "indecent." It was, said some, "insulting to the American public." Seizing the chance to make headlines, several congressmen denounced the program's participants, the radio sta-

tions that had carried the show, and the sponsor. A nationwide boycott of Chase and Sanborn coffee was subsequently proposed.

Almost everybody concerned with the program offered public apologies. The coffee company's advertising agency and the president of NBC announced their "regrets"; NBC affiliate stations were forbidden to mention either the incident or the name of Mae West on the air. Her presence on the show had thus caused a full-fledged scandal.

Despite the protests, however, Americans had remained glued to their radios during the show. *Variety*, the show-business daily, reported that, thanks to West's performance, "half the radio sets in the United States tuned in on the Edgar Bergen–Charlie McCarthy gala." When all was said and done, concluded *Variety*, it "looks like the public is not much concerned with the moral aspects of the much-vaunted case."

Many years later, Edgar Bergen laughed when he recalled the incident. "Our only mistake," he said in 1979, "was that we were 25 years ahead of our time."

Had Mae West known what she was doing when she started that furor? Absolutely. After years of being suppressed by censorship, she had deliberately loaded the show with Westian innuendo. She knew, too, that the American public was not as easily offended as it liked to pretend it was. In her autobiography, she quoted a remark made by Jim Timony.

"I wonder," the agent had said, "why these poor tormented souls, when they first detected 'sin' in your voice, Mae, didn't immediately switch off their sets." West said she "suspected that their enjoyment of my sinfulness left them with such a paralyzing sense of guilt they were only able to slough it off by hurling protests at NBC. Which they did."

Deciding to capitalize on the publicity from the radio uproar, West then embarked on a nationwide personal-appearance tour. She put together an act consisting of a male singer, an orchestra, and a group known as the Six Leading Men.

Abandoning her long-held dislike of appearing with men who towered over her, West selected only six-footers for the song-and-dance group. On stage, they wore top hats and tailcoats. She wore a clinging, full-length, black-beaded gown, a white monkey-fur jacket, an immense crown of ostrich plumes, and a dazzling assortment of diamonds.

West had, of course, performed before countless live audiences, but now she was a full-fledged Hollywood star. She played the role with gusto, delighting her audiences. Almost every performance ended with roars of approval and a standing ovation from the crowd.

When West brought the show to New York in early 1939, she was met by cheering fans and friendly reporters. One newsman asked her how she felt about censorship. "It upholds the dignity of the profession," she said with an absolutely straight face, "know what I mean?"

Returning to Hollywood in late spring 1939, West was greeted by a notable absence of movie offers. Film styles were changing; the public was now demanding "family" pictures with happy endings. After West's widely publicized problems with the censors, her condemnation by the Hearst newspapers, and the scandal produced by her radio appearance, most of the major film studios considered her unemployable.

There were, however, a few Hollywood executives who believed West could still attract moviegoers. Just as she was beginning to think about leaving the film capital to resume her stage career, she received an unusual offer. Universal Pictures was planning an offbeat film with the great comedian W. C. Fields. Would West be interested in costarring with Fields in a western spoof called *My Little Chickadee*?

West was skeptical about sharing the screen with Fields. She strongly disapproved of drinking, and Fields was not only a notorious scene-stealer but also famed for his immense consumption of alcohol. Universal's offer, however, was the only one she had, and she finally signed up to do the movie, accepting a fee of $40,000—one-tenth of what she had been paid for each of her last films.

Hoping to avoid friction with Fields, West spoke highly of him in interviews. The new movie would give Fields "a chance to do all the things he alone can do," she confided to gossip columnist Louella Parsons. "There is only one Fields," added West, "and why should I or anyone else try to change his style?" Her tone was a little different in private. "There is no one else quite like Bill [Fields]," she told a studio executive, "thank God!"

Although she claimed to have no interest in changing Fields's style, West insisted that the actor agree to "lay off all alcohol while we are shooting." She got a clause in her contract saying that she could be excused from working with him unless he was sober. Fields reportedly managed to keep away from the bottle except for one occasion. On that day, West observed that Fields was "overstimulated," and she asked the director to "pour him out of here." The director obediently approached Fields.

"Bill, you can go home," West reported him saying. "We won't need you until tomorrow morning." Fields's "puffed, bloodshot eyes gave me a side glance," West recalled. "'Ya-as,' he said with an old-world courtesy, tipping his hat to me. And he walked out with a sheepish look."

To the surprise of many Hollywood observers, West and Fields worked well together despite her obvious distrust of his habits. The final version of the film credits no writer with the story, but in fact, each of the stars wrote large sections of it. Humphrey Bogart, who was offered a role in the movie, gave his version of its authorship decades later.

"I went to the producer's office and was handed a script," recalled Bogart.

Fluttering her eyelashes and her ostrich plumes, Flower Belle Lee (West) catches the interest of Cuthbert J. Twillie (W. C. Fields) in the 1940 comedy My Little Chickadee.

"I had a few lines, then the next 30 pages would be blank except for the notation: 'Material to be supplied by Miss West.' Another few lines for me and then 30 more blank pages. 'Material to be supplied by Mr. Fields.' The whole damn script was like that. I left quietly through an open window."

My Little Chickadee tells a complicated tale about Cuthbert J. Twillie

West teases admirers in The Heat's On. *Few critics liked the 1943 film, but audiences howled over West's comic love scene with Victor Moore (center), during which he lost his toupee.*

(Fields), a con man who poses as a lawman and is hired as sheriff in a western town. West plays Flower Belle Lee, an outspoken woman who challenges local conventions and is requested to leave town. The film's centerpiece is a trial in which Flower Belle expounds West's own views about hypocritical morality. The scene expresses West's feelings about censorship and the Hays Office.

When *My Little Chickadee* was released in early 1940, the critics gave it mixed notices. Several said it would have been better if its two stars had played more scenes together. Nevertheless, it was successful, and it has remained one of the most popular and most frequently shown of all West's films. *Chickadee* contains a number of lines treasured by West fans, including "A man's kiss is his signature," and "I was in a tight spot, but I managed to wriggle out of it."

By the time *My Little Chickadee* appeared, World War II was raging in Eu-

U.S. soldiers invade France in 1944, opening the final phase of World War II. Hollywood responded to the conflict with a flood of patriotic films, none of which called for Mae West's talents.

rope. Less than two years later, the Japanese bombed the American naval base at Pearl Harbor, Hawaii, and the United States, too, was at war. Hollywood turned most of its efforts to making films about soldiers or home-front patriots, none of which were suitable vehicles for Mae West.

In 1943 she made *The Heat's On*, a comedy whose cast also included Lloyd Bridges. Some reviewers liked it; *Time* magazine, for example, said West was "still one of the most entertaining and original personalities in pictures," and "still capable of the low-minded grand manner which made *She Done*

Him Wrong (1933) a minor masterpiece." Most critics, however, considered the film a failure.

West had made 10 films in her 11 years in Hollywood and had become a legend. Despite the constraints of the censors, she had succeeded in transferring the Mae West Character from stage to screen, and she had earned the affection of millions of moviegoers. Now things had changed. When *The Heat's On* opened, *The New York Times* said, "The heat is off, but definitely." And so, it seemed, was Mae West. She would not make another movie for 27 years.

West's portrait adorns the cover of sheet music for "Diamond Lil," the popular musical's title song. West identified with all the characters she played, but "Lil" was her all-time favorite.

SEVEN

Return to the Stage

In 1943 theatrical producer Mike Todd announced that he wanted to present Mae West as Catherine the Great. Nothing could have pleased West more. She had yearned to play the famed 18th-century Russian empress for more than a decade and had even written a screenplay about her. Disappointed by the critical and box-office failure of *The Heat's On* ("I will never make a picture again," she said, "just for the sake of making a picture"), she was ready to return to the stage.

West's arrival in New York was greeted by reporters' questions about her upcoming play. "I'll say Catherine was great," she said. She confided that, after reading a dozen biographies of Catherine, she knew she was exactly the right actress to bring the colorful ruler to life. Catherine was, explained West, "the Diamond Lil of her day."

A strong and innovative sovereign,

Catherine had also been celebrated for her long list of lovers. Accordingly, Todd had planned to call his play *The Men in Her Life*. After he read about West's remarks, however, he renamed it *Catherine Was Great*. The title change was the last matter West and Todd agreed on. He envisioned a rowdy comedy, with Mae West playing Catherine as Mae West. What she had in mind was a serious historical play.

"Look Mae, forget the heavy drama," implored the producer as rehearsals began. "The audience knows you as a comedian. Don't go highbrow on them. They won't take it."

West was furious. "Take your cigar and get out of my sight!" she barked. "I was a star when you were a brick-layer!" For once in his career, the explosive Todd had met his match. Rehearsals of the *drama* proceeded.

Despite her insistence on playing

Catherine Was Great *producer Mike Todd was famed for his ability to shout down anyone who disagreed with him. He soon learned that it took more than a loud voice to subdue Mae West.*

Catherine seriously, West found it hard to stop being herself. "She had marvelous strength, great voice projection," recalled leading man Philip Huston years afterward. "She could have acted a straight part, but she [couldn't] discard the mannerisms she'd made her own. She said, 'Entah!' She could have said 'enter' like everyone else, but 'entah' was part and parcel of the public image she'd developed."

When the play opened in Philadelphia in the summer of 1943, the critics praised the star, the sets, and the costumes. The play itself, however, was attacked mercilessly. What was it, asked reviewers, a comedy or a drama? They said it left the audience feeling totally confused.

The next day, Todd stormed up to West. A cast member later reported on the scene. "Who do you think you are, Helen Hayes?" shouted Todd. "You can't act. What I want you to do is be funny. And if you don't snap out of [it] and play what you're supposed to play, you're not going to be able to get a booking in an outhouse!"

Instead of responding to Todd's outburst, West rushed to a telephone and summoned her old friend Lee Shubert. The powerful theater owner and producer showed up in Philadelphia the following day. He bought out Todd's share of the production, reduced his status to nominal producer, and gave him a blistering lecture. "If I ever hear of you talking to Miss West like that again," roared Shubert, "you'll be very fortunate to book a play of yours into a phone booth!"

Once she had gotten rid of Todd, West decided he had probably been right. The next night, she began to add comic lines to the script, and she added a curtain speech that produced a wave of laughter from the audience. "I'm glad you liked my Catherine," she said. "I like her, too. She ruled 30 million people and had 3,000 lovers. I do the best I can in two hours."

West models one of her lavish costumes from Catherine Was Great. *Convinced that the 18th-century Russian empress was "the Diamond Lil of her day," the actress had long yearned to play the role.*

Catherine Was Great went on to the Shubert Theater in New York City. Critics once again reviewed the play caustically, but the public flocked to buy tickets. The show played on Broadway for 34 weeks and then began a tour of American cities. *Variety* summed up the story: "Critics cold," said the newspaper, "but box office hot."

West followed up *Catherine* with *Ring Twice Tonight*, a very lightweight comedy in which she played an FBI agent who poses as a nightclub singer. The show opened in California and then played to enthusiastic crowds in theaters across the country. West expected her friend Lee Shubert to present it on Broadway, but after sitting through a performance, he declined. It was, he said, far too shallow and unsophisticated for New York audiences.

West was undiscouraged. "If I'm not convinced that what I do is great entertainment," she said, "I would rather do nothing at all but sit home and polish my diamonds." She did not, however, have to sit home for long. Almost as soon as *Ring Twice Tonight* closed, she was invited to star in a British production of *Diamond Lil*.

On September 11, 1947, nearly 20 years after she had first opened in *Diamond Lil* in New York, West sailed for England aboard the ocean liner *Queen Mary*. The world of the late 1940s was a very different place from the one inhabited by Diamond Lil—and by young Mae West—in the 1890s.

The intervening half-century had seen the introduction of such innovations as automobiles, airplanes, telephones, radios, and television. West, whose life had spanned these years of vast technological change, was in one sense the embodiment of both the old-fashioned and the modern. With her wigs, corsets, and long gowns, she looked like a woman of the "Gay 90s"; her uninhibited wit and sophistication, however, expressed the spirit of the post–World War II world.

Because of her movies, West was well known in England. During World War II, in fact, British pilots had named their inflatable life jackets "Mae Wests." (The use of the term, which is still listed in most dictionaries, delighted the actress. She once quipped, "I've been in *Who's Who*, and I know what's what, but it's the first time I ever made a dictionary.")

The British public, familiar with the overblown publicity about the "world's wickedest woman," was surprised and pleased by the real Mae West. "Nothing could have been less revealing or more modest than the evening gown in which Mae West greeted Southampton," one reporter wrote about her arrival in England.

After a successful tour of major British cities, West opened *Diamond Lil* in London. The raucous, colorful show was a smash hit with both critics and audiences. "Mae West is triumphant—

West autographs a "Mae West" during a visit to the set of a war movie in the mid-'70s. The actress had been delighted when World War II pilots named their inflatable life jackets after her.

she came to London last night and conquered it!" raved a typical review. The critic of the *Daily Express* wrote, "Mae West *is* entertainment. She herself is a restoration comedy rolled into one body—earthy and outspoken. Shock me? No, I just liked her."

Well-known British director Peter Glenville was among West's first British conquests. "I thought she had a sweetness of disposition and a great shyness," he recalled later. "Although she dealt with very raunchy subjects in her jokes and was a sex symbol, in her private conversations there was a certain innocence about her."

Glenville escorted West to parties where she met members of England's literary and high-society circles. For one of these affairs, hosted by wealthy writer Edith Sitwell, West wore a white, Grecian-style gown. Glenville later reported the dialogue between hostess and guest. "You look like a vestal virgin," said the distinguished and elderly Sitwell. "Baby," shot back the irrepressible West, "you don't know what you're saying!"

But, said Glenville, "for the most part, she was self-contained, a bit shy. She said a few funny things, very quietly. Watched everything. People were charmed by her." *Diamond Lil* played two shows a night to packed houses until May 1948. West, who thoroughly enjoyed this period of her life, often reminisced about her "unforgettably happy months in England."

Returning to the United States, West was met by the usual crowd of reporters. "Having spent most of my time in theaters," she observed with dry wit, "I was naturally asked what I had observed of the international situation and world problems."

After the London success of *Diamond Lil*, West was once again regarded in the United States as a strong box-office attraction. In October 1948 she was invited to reopen *Lil* at a new theater in Montclair, New Jersey.

One of the Montclair theater's producers, however, was skeptical about

West often signed pictures for fans. Part of the inscription on this one (whose recipient is unknown) reads, "This is personally from me to you with all that goes with it — which is plenty!"

booking the aging actress. Then he heard her read a few lines from the play. "I realized," said the producer, Charles Freeman, that "this gal wasn't a faded Hollywood star trading on her name. She still really had something. I knew . . . audiences would have a good time."

Freeman was right. The American revival of *Diamond Lil* opened in 1949 and kept West busy until 1951, when it finally closed after a nationwide tour. Actress Sylvia Syms was a member of the cast. "Every night," Syms later told

Once again playing her favorite character, West appears as "Diamond Lil" in 1950. "Miss West's charm," said one reviewer of the successful revival, "is unique and perennial."

had the most incredible discipline and sense of dedication in achieving it."

After each night's performance, West would leave the theater dressed in furs and jewels, wave to the crowd at the stage door, and get into her limousine as mounted policemen held back the eager fans. She and her driver would cruise around the city for a while and then, according to Syms, "she'd go back to her dressing room, have the maid put away her glamour costume, get into her slacks and babushka [head scarf], and go home."

During this run of *Diamond Lil*, a theatrical columnist asked West just how long an actress could be expected to play characters with "bounce and seductiveness." The reply was pure Mae West: "Just as long as she has her health and feels the part, and I may say that in my case, that may be almost forever.... *Diamond Lil* is all mine. I'm she. She's I, and in my modest way I consider her a classic. Like *Hamlet*, sort of, but funnier. I'm permanently typecast and I love every minute of it."

When the revival of *Diamond Lil* ended its long run, West returned to Hollywood to consider her next project. Television producers were beginning to approach her with ideas for specials and series, but she was suspicious of the new medium. "I've never liked the idea of television," she said, "because people can turn you off."

In May 1954, Jim Timony died sud-

an interviewer, "all these people lined up to get a glimpse of [West] when she came out of the stage door."

"I've never seen a more beautiful woman," continued Syms. "In her mid-fifties, Mae's skin was alabaster; her teeth were her own and absolutely beautiful.... She sold glamour, and she denly of a heart attack. He had been West's dearest friend, strongest supporter, and closest confidant for more than 30 years, and his death left her feeling more alone than she had ever been. Timony had left his law practice to be West's agent and, later, her business manager. He had been completely devoted to her. She knew there would never be anyone who could replace him.

Just as she had done when her mother died, West threw herself into activity after Timony's death. She finally accepted a television offer (to sing and dance on Dean Martin's show) and then organized a nightclub revue, which she planned to take to Las Vegas. Her new act would be really new. "All through the years," she said, "nightclubs have aimed at something for the men—girl floor shows." Now, she announced, she "was going to give women something to look at."

West designed a show with herself at the center of eight good-looking, heavily muscled bodybuilders, one of whom was the current Mr. America. She added half a dozen singers and dancers as well as her old friend, black actress and comedian Louise Beavers.

When "The Mae West Show" opened at the Sahara Hotel in Las Vegas in the summer of 1954, patrons of the gambling mecca roared their approval. Las Vegas was followed by a string of successful appearances across the coun-

West takes a bow after opening her Las Vegas act in 1954. Nightclub patrons greeted the actress and her eight handsome male costars with flowers, cheers, and demands for encores.

A quartet of former leading men — and permanent admirers — congratulate West after a nightclub performance. They are (left to right) Phil Reed, Cary Grant, Jack LaRue, and Steve Cochran.

Bodybuilder Mickey Hargitay, one-time costar in West's nightclub act, dances with Jayne Mansfield in 1956. West indignantly denied reports that she was jealous of the blond starlet.

try, including one at New York City's Latin Quarter. Here, West broke all records, outdrawing such previous moneymakers as Frank Sinatra, Sophie Tucker, and Milton Berle.

That West's public still loved her had never been clearer than on the night of the nationally televised presentation of the 1958 Academy Awards. Appearing after Shirley Jones, Betty Grable, and Rhonda Fleming, West and actor Rock Hudson delivered a sizzling rendition of "Baby, It's Cold Outside." The audience rose to its feet, laughing, whistling, and cheering as the pair cooed, crooned, hugged, and kissed their way through the song. "Mae West and Rock Hudson stopped the show cold," reported the Los Angeles *Examiner* the following day. Other press reports agreed that West had been "more radiant than ever."

Over the next several years, West updated her nightclub act, adding such current hits as "Rock Around the Clock," and replacing Mr. America with Mr. Universe, a Hungarian athlete named Mickey Hargitay. Another addition was Chester Ribonsky, a handsome, 33-year-old former wrestler from New Orleans.

When Hargitay began dating blond starlet Jayne Mansfield, reporters asked West if she was jealous. Emphatically not, said West, who even called a press conference to deny any romantic interest in Mr. Universe. Ribonsky, the new member of her troupe, was at her side as she explained that Hargitay was "only an employee." The press conference was interrupted when Hargitay, who had decided to give reporters his own views of Mae West, burst into the crowded room.

Ribonsky, who later said he thought Hargitay was about to attack him, landed a punch on the jaw of Mr. Universe. West was delighted by the resulting news stories; she knew it was good for her image to have two strong young men fighting over her.

After the fracas, West took another look at Ribonsky. He was, she concluded, not only blue-eyed, physically powerful, and good-looking; he had a gentle manner and natural intelligence that reminded her of Jim Timony. Futhermore, he clearly adored her. He soon became what West referred to as "my constant escort."

West's friends were skeptical about her new companion at first. "I think everybody expected the usual," said a choreographer who had worked with the actress for many years. "Guys who latch on to most stars are opportunists.

West gestures approvingly toward two of her "muscle men" — in this case, comedians Dean Martin (left) and Bob Hope — during rehearsals for a 1959 television special.

But [Ribonsky] was so wonderful to her, so protective, so genuinely concerned about her welfare, it was touching.... You sensed that he was not going to let anyone hurt her—ever."

In her autobiography, West noted that she had "never wanted a love that meant absorption of my whole being, surrender of my self-possession." She nevertheless decided that Ribonsky was a man who deserved "special consideration." At the age of 65, Mae West had fallen in love.

Nestled among lacy pillows in her huge, elaborate bed, West scans a fashion magazine. Although she enjoyed such publications, her sense of style was strictly her own.

EIGHT

The Last Years

Chester Ribonsky, who eventually changed his name to Paul Novak, lived with Mae West as a devoted husband in everything but name for more than 25 years. As well as being her lover and principal fan, he served as her bodyguard, chef, chauffeur, press secretary, and physical therapist. He told friends that West, 32 years older than himself, was "all the woman I'll ever want."

West had always encouraged the image of herself as a blond heartbreaker who refused to settle down with one man. Protective of that image even in her old age, she was less demonstrative in her affection than Novak. Still, it was clear that she returned his love.

When Novak was not present, West often said, "Paul's the greatest," and in a 1975 interview, she confessed that she had become "monogamous" (having only one mate). "Although I always have and always will continue looking at other men," said the 82-year-old actress, "Paul is all the man I need now. He treats me like a lady."

The two lived quietly, dividing their time between West's Hollywood apartment and her beach house near Santa Monica, California. Ever concerned about maintaining her remarkable complexion, West became increasingly unwilling to expose her skin to direct sunlight or seawater. For outdoor exercise, she and Novak took late-night strolls and sometimes went wading in the surf.

Novak did his best to regulate his companion's lifelong passion for sweets, especially after tests revealed that she had diabetes. When she developed cataracts in both eyes, he arranged for the surgery that restored her sight. Respecting West's desire to appear in perfect physical condition, he carefully kept the operation a secret

When silent-movie queen Gloria Swanson introduced West at a 1963 banquet, West brought down the house. "If there's anything you want to know," she told the former superstar, "just ask."

from the public. "I believe I was put on this earth," he once said, "to take care of Mae West."

As soon as West had recovered from her cataract surgery, Novak encouraged her to accept an invitation from the University of Southern California, which was organizing an elaborate salute to the film industry. Mistress of ceremonies was to be Gloria Swanson, one of the most glamorous screen stars of the 1920s.

After Swanson had introduced West during the program, she joked, "I used to think I was something of a sex sym-

bol until Mae West came along." The room echoed with laughter and cheers when West smiled at the legendary Swanson and said, "If there's anything you want to know, just ask."

A year later, West suffered a minor heart attack, which kept her at home for several months. Until she felt and looked her best, she refused to be seen in public, but by early 1965 she was feeling well enough to grant an interview to society columnist Cobina Wright.

"She looks wonderful," reported Wright. "I have always felt that Mae only kids sex and is really a very spiritual woman. Let's hope that one of the greatest phenomena in show-business history is soon fully recovered and amusing us once more with her wonderful quips."

By 1966 West was back in shape and hard at work on her newest venture, a rock-and-roll album to be called *Way Out West*. In the 60s, with rebellious young people expressing new ideas and challenging old authority, a new kind of music was emerging. A lifelong rebel herself, West felt completely comfortable with the songs of Bob Dylan and the Beatles, which she recorded in her usual sultry style. *Way Out West* sold a respectable 100,000 copies and was followed by *Wild Christmas*, a Westian version of traditional yuletide music.

When West turned 75 in 1968, the

Paul Novak, West's devoted companion during the last decades of her life, keeps an affectionate eye on her as she conducts an animated conversation with director George Cukor (left).

University of Southern California gave her an elaborate birthday party. Preparing for the event as for any performance, she picked out props from the 20th Century-Fox property department, selected a dazzling costume, and rehearsed her act.

For her musical numbers, West chose "Doin' the Grizzly Bear," which she had first performed in 1910, and "Frankie and Johnny," dating from her *Diamond Lil* of 1928. She responded to the crowd's standing ovation by saying, "I want to thank you for your generous applause—and your very heavy breathing."

Reporting on the occasion, the press went wild. One writer began his account by announcing, "I'm in love with Mae West all over again." Pictures of her and stories about her "beauty secrets" began to appear in newspapers and magazines across the country. *Life* magazine ran a splashy story on her, devoting its cover to a shot of West and her pet monkey posed on a huge bed beneath a mirrored ceiling. The public—and the Hollywood producers—were reminded that Mae West was still a star.

West had not made a movie in 27 years. She had received film proposals but, disliking the scripts or the terms on which they were extended, she had turned them all down. In 1970, however, she was offered a starring role in *Myra Breckenridge*, and she accepted it. Based on a best-selling novel by Gore Vidal, the film dealt with America's hypocrisy and confusion about sex, a subject close to West's heart.

Costarring with West in *Myra Breckenridge* were Raquel Welch and Farrah Fawcett, but when the film opened in New York City, it was clear that the crowds had come to see only one woman. As West's limousine slowly approached Broadway's Criterion Theater, a mass of screaming fans—estimated by one police officer to be the biggest crowd to assemble since World War II—surrounded it, pulling on its doors and straining to see its occupant.

Gowned in a white, feather-trimmed silk sheath, West slowly emerged from

West talks about Myra Breckenridge *at a 1969 press conference. Originally offered $100,000 to appear in the film, she had scornfully declined. She demanded — and got — $350,000.*

her car and entered the theater with 10 tall male escorts. Her admirers screamed and shoved, hoping to get close to her. A small army of patrolmen and mounted troopers did their best to prevent a full-scale riot, but several injuries were reported. One middle-aged man was led away in hysterics, shouting, "I *touched* Mae West!"

Critical reviews of *Myra Breckenridge* were uniformly dreadful, but West remained the woman of the hour. The morning after the premiere, 200 reporters converged on her hotel for a press conference. West was in her ele-ment, trading wisecracks and cheer-fully posing for endless photographs.

A round of parties and celebrations followed the opening. At one of them, West ran into Cary Grant, who was once again awed by his old friend's immense vitality. "She's such a glorious burst of energy!" he said later. "Always was. Always will be." West even received an invitation to dine at the White House. She declined. "That seems like an awful long way to go for just one meal," she told friends.

Revived interest in the durable star resulted in a series of "Mae West festivals" on television stations all over the United States. West resented the fact that most local stations showed her films in shortened form, but she was happy that new audiences were seeing them, and she was gratified by her sudden popularity among the young.

As West aged, she began to show signs of eccentricity. She insisted, for example, on going to bed in full makeup in case a fire in her apartment building forced her to make an unscheduled midnight appearance. Nevertheless, her sense of humor remained sharp.

She was known to disapprove of newsstand pornography, but in the early 1970s, she agreed to accept $25,000 from a popular "skin" magazine for a nude centerfold picture. The publisher was delighted until he realized she expected him to use a 40-year-

West accepts a bouquet from her Myra Breckenridge *costar, Raquel Welch. Said Welch, "Roses mean affection." Sniffed West later, "Roses also mean a damn good publicity shot. I can read her mind."*

old painting of her. "Why bother with all the posing?" she asked with a straight face. "After all, I haven't changed." The publisher found another subject for his centerfold.

In early 1976 talk-show host Dick Cavett asked West to appear on his upcoming television special. He would interview her and then she would sing two numbers. West said she would agree to appear in a 15-minute segment for $25,000, and Cavett quickly signed her up.

As usual, West wanted to prepare for her performance, but Cavett, following his regular practice, refused to show her his interview questions before the show. West was annoyed, but in 70 years of show business, she had never broken a contract, and she would not break one now.

The interview went smoothly enough, but West clearly had trouble remembering the director's instructions during her renditions of "Frankie and Johnny" and "After You've Gone." Following several false starts, however, she produced a classic performance that drew a long round of spontaneous applause from the studio crew. The show's reviewers shared the crew's sentiments.

After saying that as a "reasonable observer" he had expected the aging West to be "grotesque," the *New York Times* critic wrote, "But reason somehow seems puny when confronted with Miss West. She is something—a wonderful, glamorous, talented, and marvelously witty something—unto herself."

Two years after the Cavett show, West agreed to appear in *Sextette*, a new film comedy. Also featured were Tony Curtis, Timothy Dalton, George Hamilton, Dom DeLuise, Ringo Starr, Alice Cooper, and Keith Moon.

Starr later admitted he had been "uptight" about the prospect of performing with West. "But by the end of the second day," said the former Beatle, "I would have stayed on as long as she wanted me. She's old enough to be my grandmother, so it's sort of embarrassing to say, but she's bloody attractive."

One of *Sextette*'s production managers later told an interviewer that when he first saw West on the set he thought she was "pathetic." He said she "looked like a little old lady just getting through the night." Then filming began. "The minute they hit the lights," he said, "she became the magic woman we know."

Sextette, in which the 85-year-old West played the bride of youthful Timothy Dalton, was not a success. Many reviewers were violent in their denunciation of the film and its star. *The New York Times* compared West to "a plump sheep that's been stood on its hind legs [and] dressed in a drag queen's idea of chic," and called *Sextette* "a disorienting freak show." Another New York review derided the film as "a monument of ghoulish camp."

Some sentimental reviewers, however, gave *Sextette* cautious praise. It would, suggested the *Los Angeles Times*, "be cherished by her fans, for whom it was made." The Los Angeles *Herald-Examiner* said "the lady seems as indestructible as the Statue of Liberty and well worth a visit." *Time* magazine pronounced the movie "so bad" that it was "good, an instant classic."

Novak did his best to keep the bad reviews out of West's hands, but she was shrewd enough to understand that *Sextette* was a failure. Nevertheless, she optimistically predicted that it would, like *The Rocky Horror Picture Show*, become a cult film whose fans would watch it repeatedly.

In August 1980, one week before her 87th birthday, West fell out of bed. Novak helped her to a chair and brought her a cup of tea. She tried to talk, but found she was unable to form coherent words, and she began to cry. She had suffered a stroke.

Novak did everything he could over the next few months to comfort her and restore her health. He stayed with her 24 hours a day, sleeping for a few hours each night in a cot at the foot of her bed. He hired a faith healer, ran her old films, played her record albums. All his efforts were in vain.

When West developed chills on November 22, 1980, Novak called the nearest church—which happened to be Catholic—and asked for a clergyman to come at once. Although West was not a Catholic, she seemed to find comfort in the blessing the priest gave her. She died peacefully moments after he left her bedside.

Before West's body was sent home to Brooklyn to be interred next to her mother's, Novak arranged for a small funeral service in Hollywood. Producer Ross Hunter was among those who spoke. He noted that West "had an absorption that seemed to border on the total," but that "the more she concentrated on Mae West, the more she gave to others." He also saluted West's relationship with Novak, which he called "a singularly tender love story in which she had been caught up for more than a quarter of a century."

The close friends who attended the service agreed that West would have enjoyed it; instead of the usual somber music, the air was filled with such songs as "Frankie and Johnny" and "My Old Flame." As Hunter put it, "The Mae West Character never wanted anyone to feel sorry for her and she wouldn't want them to start now."

West was, as one old friend described her after her death, "a woman of many paradoxes, complications, and contradictions." She was ambitious, acquisitive, fond of luxury and compliments; she was also sympathetic and enormously generous. Carefully maintaining her hard-as-diamonds image, she was almost furtive about her acts of kindness, but reports of her openhandedness were widely circulated among the theatrical community.

Harold Gary, an actor who had known West for years, gave an interviewer an example, that of Pearl Regay, a onetime top musical star. Regay,

Long known for her appreciation of bodybuilding, West presents the 1977 Mr. America trophy to Dave Johns, a Los Angeles County juvenile probation officer.

"who was down on her luck," said Gary, "told me Mae paid all of her bills and never let anybody know it. And old fighters held her in high regard for her financial help. She was like a queen to them."

The Mae West Character smoked, drank, and often engaged in rowdy dialogue. The offstage West never used tobacco or alcohol and was deeply

West receives birthday kisses from a pair of young admirers in 1977. The 84-year-old actress amused well-wishers by observing, "I always say, everything good happens after dark!"

offended by vulgar language. She delighted in defying convention, demanded the right to live her own life as she saw fit, and made no secret of her many romantic relationships. Nevertheless, she had her own rules of propriety.

When publicists scheduled her for a photo session with Katharine Hepburn in 1970, West astonished them by refusing to meet her fellow actress. "I never cared much for that party," said West. "You know she lived with a married man for years."

Despite such quirky displays of puritanism, West had never had any patience with society's double standard for men and women. She had grown up in a world that smiled or looked the other way at male sexual promiscuity,

at the same time condemning any woman whose actions were less than "pure." West regarded such attitudes as utterly hypocritical, a judgment she also applied to most censorship.

She rejected the idea that a few members of society had the right to impose their own concept of morality on the rest of the world. She lost many of her battles against censorship, but she never gave up trying to outwit the self-elected guardians of public morals. She conceded that sex was "the basic theme of all my plays and pictures," but she insisted that she treated the subject "with humor and good nature, rather than as something shameful"— a claim with which few people would disagree today.

Although West reveled in her image as the "world's wickedest woman," her private ideas about sex were far from flamboyant. They are perhaps best expressed in a letter she wrote to Dr. Alfred Kinsey, the distinguished author of such books as *Sexual Behavior in the Human Male.*

"I feel as an actress and playwright I have been frank and honest in dealing with the subject [of sex]—as I know you have been as a scientist," said West to Kinsey. "I believe the more we are prepared to accept sex in our lives without a distorting sense of guilt and fear, the less tragic will be any of its consequences.

"I would be the last to encourage

uncontrolled sexual activity, licentiousness, in anyone. Obviously, early and thorough sex education and intelligent and sympathetic religious guidance are needed to enable men and women to accept and adjust the patterns of their sex lives so they may experience their basic human needs with dignity and self-respect.

"Perhaps, Dr. Kinsey, you will say all this doesn't sound like Mae West talking—not the Mae West of the worldwide publicized sex personality. It happens to be Mae West thinking out loud."

The world will remember West for her witty one-liners: "When I'm good, I'm very good, but when I'm bad, I'm better"; "Too much of a good thing can be wonderful"; "I used to be Snow White, but I drifted"; "Between two evils, I always pick the one I never tried before." People who knew her will remember her many generous acts—in spite of her efforts to conceal them. Moviegoers will continue to laugh over such West classics as *She Done Him Wrong* and *My Little Chickadee*.

But Mae West should also be remembered for the joy she found in life, for her unquenchable vitality, and for her insistence on being the woman she

Admirers surround the "Mae West Character" in Goin' to Town. *"Mae West," an astute critic once said, "is her own best invention and no one believes it or enjoys it more than she herself."*

wanted to be. In her own world, and on her own terms, she was indeed one of the century's "greatest phenomena."

FURTHER READING

Eells, George, and Stanley Musgrove. *Mae West.* New York: William Morrow, 1982.

Haskell, Molly. *From Reverence to Rape: The Treatment of Women in the Movies.* New York: Holt, Rinehart and Winston, 1973.

Mordden, Ethan. *Movie Star: A Look at the Women Who Made Hollywood.* New York: St. Martin's Press, 1983.

Rosen, Marjorie. *Popcorn Venus.* New York: Avon, 1974.

West, Mae. *Goodness Had Nothing to Do With It.* New York: Belvedere Publishers, 1981.

CHRONOLOGY

Aug. 17, 1893	Born Mary Jane West in Brooklyn, New York
1900	Appears in first amateur performance
1901–04	Performs with Gotham Theater stock company
1908–09	Tours with comedian William Hogan
1911	Marries Frank Wallace
	Appears in musical, *A La Broadway*
1912	West's show in New Haven is closed by censors
1913–17	West tours on the vaudeville circuit
1926–27	Writes and stars in Broadway play, *Sex*
1927	Arrested and briefly jailed for "producing an immoral show"
1928	Opens in *Diamond Lil*
Jan. 26, 1930	West's mother, Matilda, dies
1931	West opens in a dramatization of her 1931 novel, *The Constant Sinner;* the play closes after she refuses to eliminate interracial scenes
1932	Makes first movie, *Night After Night*
1933	Stars in *She Done Him Wrong* and *I'm No Angel*
1934	Stars in *Belle of the Nineties*
1936	Stars in *Klondike Annie* and *Go West, Young Man*
1937	Makes a controversial appearance on radio's "Chase and Sanborn Hour"
1940	Stars in *My Little Chickadee*
1942	Divorces Frank Wallace
1943	Returns to the stage in *Catherine Was Great*
1948–51	Brings revival of *Diamond Lil* to London and cities across the United States
1954	Begins touring with a nightclub act
1958	Begins relationship with Chester Ribonsky (Paul Novak)
1959	Publishes autobiography, *Goodness Had Nothing to Do With It*
1966	Records her first record album, *Way Out West*
1968	Attends a 75th birthday gala in her honor at the University of Southern California
1970	Co stars in *Myra Breckenridge*
1978	Appears in the film comedy *Sextette*
Nov. 22, 1980	Dies at home in California

INDEX

A La Broadway, 33, 54, 55
Academy Awards, 94
amateur shows, 23, 24, 25
Ameche, Don, 79
Apollo Theater, 70
Armstrong, Louis, 78
Barrymore, Ethel, 47
Beatles, the, 98, 102
Beavers, Louise, 93
Belle of the Nineties, 69, 70, 72
Bergen, Edgar, 79, 81
Berle, Milton, 94
Bible, 45, 80
Bogart, Humphrey, 82
bootleggers, 39, 40
Breen, Joseph, 58, 60
Bridges, Lloyd, 85
Bright, John, 58
Broadway, 32, 39, 41, 43, 48, 51, 57, 61, 89, 99
Brooklyn, 19, 21, 22, 23, 26, 30, 74, 78, 102
California, 70, 71, 89, 97
Catherine Was Great, 87, 89
Cavett, Dick, 101
censorship, 16, 33, 40, 41, 57, 67, 69, 70, 72, 73, 77, 79, 81, 82, 84, 85, 104
"Chase and Sanborn Hour," 79
Chicago, 48, 49, 70
Clarendon, Hal, 26
Cohen, Emanuel, 77, 78, 79
Colette, Sidonie-Gabrielle, 16
Columbia Theater, 32
Constant Sinner, The, 49, 51
Cox, James, 39
Criterion Theater, 99
critics, 29, 33, 42, 47, 62, 66, 70, 73, 84, 88, 89, 90, 101

Dalton, Timothy, 101, 102
Davies, Marion, 76
Depression, the, 48, 50
Diamond Lil, 21, 47, 48, 53, 57, 58, 89, 90, 91, 92, 99
Dietrich, Marlene, 13
Drag, The, 43, 45
Edison, Thomas Alva, 13
Ellington, Duke, 69
England, 89, 90, 91
Every Day's a Holiday, 78, 79
Fawcett, Farrah, 99
Fields, W. C., 82, 83, 84
Films of Mae West, The (Tuska), 67
Fleming, Rhonda, 94
Ford, Helen, 37
Freeman, Charles, 91
Garbo, Greta, 13
Garvey, Lou, 34
Gary, Harold, 103
Glenville, Peter, 90, 91
Go West, Young Man, 77
Goin' to Town, 72, 73
Gone With the Wind, 63
Goodness Had Nothing to Do With It, 23
Gotham Theater, 26
Grable, Betty, 94
Grant, Cary, 58, 61, 67, 100
Hamlet, 45, 92
Harding, Warren G., 39
Hargitay, Mickey, 94, 95
Harlem, 63
Harlow, Jean, 13
Hathaway, Henry, 77, 78
Hayes, Helen, 88
Hays, Will, 57, 58, 67, 76
Hays Office, 57, 58, 60, 67, 69, 72, 76, 79, 84

Hearst, William Randolph, 76, 77, 82
Heat's On, The, 85, 87
Hepburn, Katharine, 104
Hogan, Willie, 26, 27, 29
Hollywood, 13, 14, 16, 51, 53, 54, 57, 58,
    61, 62, 63, 64, 67, 69, 71, 72, 79, 81,
    82, 85, 91, 92, 97, 99, 103
Hudson, Rock, 94
Hunter, Ross, 103
Huston, Philip, 88
I'm No Angel, 61, 64, 66, 67, 69
jazz, 39, 47, 69, 78
Jazz Singer, The, 51
Jolson, Al, 51
Kaufman, Al, 57
Kinsey, Dr. Alfred, 104, 105
Klondike Annie, 75, 76
Klotman, Phyllis, 63
Las Vegas, 93
Latin Quarter, 94
Le Baron, William, 54, 58
Life, 99
Lives of a Bengal Lancer, 77
London, 90, 91
Los Angeles, 64
Lumière, Auguste, 13
Lumière, Louis, 13
Mae West look, 72
"Mae West Show, The," 93
Mae Wests, 90
Mansfield, Jayne, 94
Martin, Dean, 93
McCarthy, Charlie, 79, 81
McDaniel, Hattie, 63
McKee, Joseph, 45
Men in Her Life, The, 87
Metro-Goldwyn-Mayer, 13
Mr. America, 93, 94
Mr. Universe, 94, 95
Montclair, New Jersey, 91
Moral Producing Company, The, 42
Motion Picture Producers and
    Distributors of America, 57

Motion Picture Relief Fund, 62
My Little Chickadee, 82, 83, 84, 105
Myra Breckenridge, 99, 100
Nation, The, 66
National Legion of Decency, 57
NBC, 80, 81
New York City, 13, 29, 30, 32, 33, 34, 39,
    42, 45, 47, 48, 49, 51, 53, 54, 56, 63,
    67, 78, 81, 87, 89, 94, 99, 102
New York Times, The, 33, 42, 47, 85, 101,
    102
Night After Night, 53, 54, 56, 57
Novak, Paul, 97, 98, 102, 103
    see also Ribonsky, Chester
Palace Theater, 33, 34, 51
Paramount Pictures, 13, 53, 54, 57, 62,
    64, 67, 71, 72, 76, 77
Paris, 13, 78
Parsons, Louella, 53, 82
Pickford, Mary, 14
Popcorn Venus (Rosen), 14
Producing Managers' Association, 40,
    41, 42, 57
Prohibition, 39, 40
Queen Mary, 89
radio, 29, 39, 58, 79, 80, 81, 82, 90
Raft, George, 53, 55, 56, 57
Regay, Pearl, 103
Ribonsky, Chester, 94, 95, 97
    see also Novak, Paul
Ring Twice Tonight, 89
Roaring Twenties, 37
Rocky Horror Picture Show, The, 102
Rosen, Marjorie, 14
Royal Theater, 23, 24, 25
Salvation Army, 61
Savoy, Bert, 47
Schenck, Joe, 27
Scott, Randolph, 77
segregation, 49, 50
"Sepia Mae West," 72
Sex, 41, 42, 45
Sextette, 101, 102

Sexual Behavior in the Human Male, 104
She Done Him Wrong, 57, 58, 60, 61, 62, 63, 64, 70, 85, 105
Shubert, Lee, 88, 89
silent movies, 39, 51, 53
Sinatra, Frank, 94
Sitwell, Edith, 91
Six Leading Men, the, 81
Skipworth, Alison, 55, 56
Society for the Suppression of Vice, 43
Sometime, 37
Southampton, 90
speakeasies, 39
Stark, Mabel, 64
Starr, Ringo, 101, 102
Stromberg, Hunt, 72
Stromberg, Kitty, 72
Sumner, John, 43
Swanson, Gloria, 98
Syms, Sylvia, 91, 92
Taylor, Libby, 63
television, 29, 79, 90, 92, 93, 100, 101
Thomas, Bill, 57, 62
Thompson, Marion Spitzer, 15
Timony, Jim, 41, 42, 43, 45, 49, 63, 70, 71, 81, 92, 93, 95
Todd, Mike, 87, 88
Troy, William, 66
Tucker, Lorenzo, 49, 51
Tucker, Sophie, 94
Tuska, Jon, 67
20th Century-Fox, 99
Universal Pictures, 13, 14, 82
University of Southern California, 98, 99
Valentino, Rudolph, 53
Variety, 48, 81, 89
vaudeville, 24, 25, 26, 29, 31, 37, 39, 41, 51, 53
Victoria, queen of England, 19
Vidal, Gore, 99
Walker, James J., 45
Wallace, Frank, 29, 30, 31, 32, 73, 74, 75

Warner Brothers, 53
Watts, "Professor," 23
Way Out West, 98
Wayburn, Ned, 32, 33
Welch, Raquel, 99
West, John Edwin (brother), 23
West, John Patrick (father), 21, 22, 24, 25, 71, 74
West, Mary Jane (Mae)
  amateur shows, 23, 24, 25, 26
  arrested, 45, 46, 47
  birth, 19
  death, 13, 102
  divorce, 31, 75
  early years, 19–27
  later years, 97–105
  lovers, 15, 27, 64, 95
  "Mae West Character," 15, 16, 31, 51, 55, 61, 71, 79, 85, 103, 105
  marriage, 30, 73, 74
  mother's death and, 49
  moves to Holywood, 53–54
  nightclub act, 93, 94
  as playwright, 41, 42, 43, 47, 58, 104
  press campaign against, 76, 77, 92
  relationship with Paul Novak, 95, 97, 98, 102, 103
  tours with act, 26, 27, 29, 30, 33, 34, 37, 48, 81, 91
  writes novel, 49
West, Matilda "Tillie" Delker Doelger (mother), 19, 20, 21, 23, 27, 41, 48, 49, 74
West, Mildred "Beverly" (sister), 23
Wicked Age, The, 47
Wild Christmas, 98
women's movement, 15
World War I, 37, 42
World War II, 84, 90, 99
Wright, Cobina, 98
Yale, 34
Ziegfeld, Florenz, 32
Ziegfeld *Follies*, 32

PICTURE CREDITS

Carol Bergman, a media consultant and critic, is a member of the Media Studies faculty at the New School for Social Research. She has a regular column in *Family Circle* magazine, and has written articles for *The New York Times, Cineaste, American History Illustrated, Ms.,* and *Woman's World.*

❖　❖　❖

Matina S. Horner is president of Radcliffe College and associate professor of psychology and social relations at Harvard University. She is best known for her studies of women's motivation, achievement, and personality development. Dr. Horner serves on several national boards and advisory councils, including those of the National Science Foundation, Time Inc., and the Women's Research and Education Institute. She earned her B. A. from Bryn Mawr College and Ph.D. from the University of Michigan, and holds honorary degrees from many colleges and universities, including Mount Holyoke, Smith, Tufts, and the University of Pennsylvania.